GROUPWORK PRACTICE
FOR SOCIAL WORKERS

SAGE | 50 YEARS

SAGE was founded in 1965 by Sara Miller McCune to support the dissemination of usable knowledge by publishing innovative and high-quality research and teaching content. Today, we publish more than 750 journals, including those of more than 300 learned societies, more than 800 new books per year, and a growing range of library products including archives, data, case studies, reports, conference highlights, and video. SAGE remains majority-owned by our founder, and after Sara's lifetime will become owned by a charitable trust that secures our continued independence.

Los Angeles | London | Washington DC | New Delhi | Singapore

GROUPWORK PRACTICE FOR SOCIAL WORKERS

KARIN CRAWFORD, MARIE PRICE AND BOB PRICE

SAGE

Los Angeles | London | New Delhi
Singapore | Washington DC

Los Angeles | London | New Delhi
Singapore | Washington DC

SAGE Publications Ltd
1 Oliver's Yard
55 City Road
London EC1Y 1SP

SAGE Publications Inc.
2455 Teller Road
Thousand Oaks, California 91320

SAGE Publications India Pvt Ltd
B 1/I 1 Mohan Cooperative Industrial Area
Mathura Road
New Delhi 110 044

SAGE Publications Asia-Pacific Pte Ltd
3 Church Street
#10-04 Samsung Hub
Singapore 049483

Editor: Kate Wharton
Editorial assistant: Laura Walmsley
Production editor: Katie Forsythe
Copyeditor: Jennifer Hinchliffe
Proofreader: Clare Weaver
Indexer: Laura Knox
Marketing manager: Camille Richmond
Cover design: Lisa Harper-Wells
Typeset by: C&M Digitals (P) Ltd, Chennai, India
Printed in Great Britain by Henry Ling Limited at
The Dorset Press, Dorchester, DT1 1HD

Library of Congress Control Number: 2014941225

British Library Cataloguing in Publication data

A catalogue record for this book is available from
the British Library

MIX
Paper from
responsible sources
FSC
www.fsc.org   FSC™ C013985

ISBN 978-1-4462-0886-1
ISBN 978-1-4462-0887-8 (pbk)

At SAGE we take sustainability seriously. Most of our products are printed in the UK using FSC papers and boards.
When we print overseas we ensure sustainable papers are used as measured by the Egmont grading system.
We undertake an annual audit to monitor our sustainability.

TABLE OF CONTENTS

ACKNOWLEDGEMENTS

Firstly we would like to begin by thanking Karin for putting her faith in us and bringing us on board during the course of this collaboration. Secondly a big thank you goes out to Laura, Kate and Katie from Sage for putting up with our questions, stretching deadlines and providing resolute support to us throughout the various stages. Lastly we would like to acknowledge the tolerance and patience of our family and friends who accepted with good faith our hermit lifestyle for a six-month period whilst we wrote this book – you were always in our thoughts.

Bob and Marie Price

PART I

GROUPWORK IN CONTEXT

1

INTRODUCING GROUPWORK

Chapter summary

In this chapter you will learn about

- the overall purpose, aims, scope and features of this book
- how the book is structured and the brief contents of each chapter
- how the book is aligned with a range of national standards and requirements related to professional social work education and practice
- the key themes that underpin the whole book
- the range of terms, words and phrases used to describe groupwork

---

INTRODUCTION

Groups are the basic expressions of human relationships; in them lies the greatest power of man. To try to work with them in a disciplined way is like trying to harness the power of the elements and includes the same kind of scientific thinking, as well as serious consideration of ethics. Like atomic power, groups can be harmful and helpful. To work with such power is a humbling and difficult task. (Konopka, 1963: vii–viii)

Social work practitioners work with groups of people in many different ways and in many different contexts. Whilst some of the wording in the above quotation may reflect the date it was written, some fifty years ago, it powerfully reflects the complexity of challenges and opportunities that may arise in contemporary groupwork practice. This book sets out to help you, the reader, understand and develop the knowledge, skills and values that are required to practise effectively in this complex context. In exploring groupwork for social workers who work with adults and children across a whole range of needs, this book takes a generic approach.

This introductory chapter will provide you with an overview of the whole book, laying out its purpose, aims and scope through an outline of the structure, key themes and learning features. This chapter will also identify how the contents of this book are related to key national standards and requirements for social work practice and education. As an introduction to your learning across the book, this chapter can be likened to a course induction process. Given the significance of language, terminology and discourse to how we understand and interpret the world around us, in order to inform your studies through the book, this chapter also includes discussion about the different definitions and understanding of the terms 'group' and 'groupwork'.

Despite the acknowledged complexity and powerful opportunities offered through effective groupwork, there has been recognition over a number of years that this aspect of practice is at times perceived as marginal, out-of-date (Doel and Sawden, 1999) and of less value or importance than other aspects of practice, particularly those underpinned by procedural and managerial drivers (Preston-Shoot, 2007). It is our intention through this text to further your understanding of the value of working with groups and thereby to raise the profile of groupwork practice as one of many aspects of effective professional social work intervention. By engaging with the materials in this book you will be able to develop your knowledge, skills and values for groupworking in the complex interprofessional care and support environment. Throughout the chapters there is an emphasis on the experience of group members and how they can fully and meaningfully participate in all aspects of the group process. This chapter summarises how the two parts of this book address theoretical, practical and methodological concerns, alongside thematic foci on empowerment, user participation and professional development.

BOOK STRUCTURE

This book is set out in two parts; the first part, Chapters 1, 2 and 3, set the context, background and theoretical approaches that underpin an understanding of groupwork practice in social work. The second part of the book, Chapters 4, 5, 6, 7 and 8, builds on this knowledge, exploring practice skills and directly discussing groupwork practice. The chapters that make up this second, practice-orientated part of the book are structured to address the 'life course', or processes, of working with a group. The final chapter will summarise the book in a way that helps you to focus on your development as a social work practitioner. Thus, by incorporating theory and practice, with interactive content throughout, the book provides a practice guide to support you in developing your skills, knowledge and approach to working with groups. Each of the chapters is briefly summarised below. As well as addressing key national standards for social work, including the Professional Capabilities Framework, as you read and study this book, you will become aware of recurring **key themes** that are threaded throughout the text of each chapter. These themes are:

- Values and ethics, anti-oppressive practice, empowerment – use of power;
- The development of practice skills and evidence-based practice;
- Multi-agency and interprofessional working with others in groups;
- The service-user experience and opportunity for participation in all processes of group-work development;
- Professional development, evaluation of practice, reflective and reflexive practice.

Chapter 2

This chapter sets the background and current context of groupwork in social work practice. It includes some brief historical perspectives and contemporary examples of groupworking, including models of groupwork. Thus the chapter will discuss the professional context of groupwork, also exploring where the concept of groupwork practice interrelates with the work of other professionals, including community work. The chapter gives a broad overview of the tasks and responsibilities of the groupworker and consideration of groupwork as a social work intervention; this is then further developed in Chapters 4–7. The chapter will also introduce you to some of the different types of groups that you may work with in social work practice.

Chapter 3

As the final chapter in Part I of the book, Chapter 3 provides an overview of the theoretical context of groupwork practice as it explores some examples of theories that might be used to aid understanding and practice with groups. Essentially a chapter in two parts, the first part of Chapter 3 examines theories that explain group development; behaviours in groups and group processes; descriptive theories. The second part of the chapter moves on to explore theories that can inform practice interventions through groupwork; prescriptive theories. The separation of descriptive and prescriptive theories in this way is a purely artificial one that aids structure and understanding through the text, as the two parts have significant overlap in that descriptive theories commonly inform prescriptive theory and thereby both are influential on groupwork practice.

Chapter 4

Chapter 4 is the first chapter in the second part of the book, where each chapter will draw on earlier learning from Part I, but will focus on practice skills, knowledge, ethics and values. The chapters in this section follow the 'life course' of working with a group, with this first chapter setting the foundation by exploring practice in preparing for groupwork. Central to this chapter are planning processes, in particular the chapter considers how service users may be supported to participate in planning groupwork and the importance of planning, at this early stage, for evaluation of the whole process. As part of the planning work, the chapter encourages you to consider a range of practical issues, such as the setting and resources needed, as well as preparing for how to address complex issues related to inter-group and intra-group relations. The chapter will also consider how contemporary developments in social networking and the use of information technology have influenced or can support groupwork practice.

Chapter 5

Moving on from the groundwork set out in the previous chapter, Chapter 5 explores the specific practice skills, knowledge, values and ethics needed when initiating groupwork. In particular, in this chapter you will learn about the important first session and the roles and responsibilities of practitioners in groupwork. Through your studies in this chapter you will develop your understanding of intergroup relationships, including consideration of issues of authority, control and power between group participants and groupworkers, and how you might manage these. The chapter also addresses the practicalities of process and content, in particular setting aims and objectives, achieving group consensus and establishing roles. Within this, you will also reflect on the role of Information Technology as an aid in the groupwork process and how the skills and tools you need as a groupworker may differ when setting up and facilitating virtual groups.

Chapter 6

In Chapter 6 you will read about a range of important practice considerations for groupwork practitioners supporting the core phase of groupwork intervention. In particular, the chapter draws on theory from Chapter 3 to support your understanding of behaviours in groups, group development, critical incidents and the different techniques, tools and activities that you can draw upon in response to different circumstances. The chapter explores the important roles and purposes of formative review, monitoring and recording, and how through this and other professional processes, such as supervision, you will gain professional support, guidance and development as a groupwork practitioner.

Chapter 7

As the final chapter in Part II the 'practice' section of the book, Chapter 7 will consider the final phases of working with a group, in particular addressing issues of 'closure' and ending. This is a key phase of the overall groupwork process and the chapter will address the significance of working through 'closure' and 'what next'; engaging service users meaningfully in the process of groupwork review and evaluation will be a core focus of this discussion. By further developing your knowledge and skills in relation to evaluation, outcomes, recording, reporting, service-user participation, using supervision and support, this chapter builds on and consolidates your learning across all of the previous chapters in this book.

Chapter 8

With a focus on your development as a social work practitioner and groupworker, this final chapter of the book effectively summarises the book and draws out the book's core themes, as set out earlier. Chapter 8 will also review how your learning across the book will have supported you in meeting national standards for social work practice including the Professional Capabilities Framework. Through reflective questions, activities, practical tasks, tools and guidance, the chapter emphasises the enhancement of practice, particularly reflective and reflexive practice.

ALIGNMENT WITH NATIONAL REQUIREMENTS FOR SOCIAL WORK

As you study the chapters in this book, your learning and development will be closely linked to national requirements for professional social work practice; these are highlighted throughout the chapters within the content, activities and resources.

Professional capabilities framework for social workers

In particular the book has been written to reflect the domains of The Professional Capabilities Framework for Social Workers (PCF), particularly the three levels applicable to social work students: readiness for direct practice; the end of the first placement; and the end of the qualifying program. The PCF was developed by the Social Work Reform Board and is available from The College of Social Work (www. collegeofsocialwork.org). A diagram of the PCF, known as the 'fan diagram' is provided at the back of this book, however, for ease of reference, the nine domains are provided below with a brief overview of how they are addressed within the chapters of this book.

Professionalism – identify and behave as a professional social worker, committed to professional development

This book is underpinned by a commitment to professionalism, in particular the whole basis of the text is to support you in developing a professional, knowledgeable, skilful, ethical and responsible approach to groupwork in social work. As a learning text, each chapter is written to support your professional development, with Chapter 8 having a specific focus on enhancing groupwork practice.

Values and ethics – apply social work ethical principles and values to guide professional practice

Social work values and ethical principles are reflected in the core themes of the book, particularly with regards to professional values, anti-oppressive practice, empowerment and service-user participation within groupwork practice. As such this domain is embedded throughout all of the book's chapters.

Diversity – recognise diversity and apply anti-discriminatory and anti-oppressive principles in practice

The principles of diversity are again reflected throughout the text and the core themes. In order to support your learning and recognise the value of diversity, across the book there are examples and discussion about groupwork practice with a range of service users in different service contexts, for example, work with children, in mental health settings, with users who have learning disabilities, domestic violence etc.

Rights, justice and economic wellbeing – advance human rights and promote social justice and economic wellbeing

The fundamental principles of human rights, justice, wellbeing and equality are embedded within social work's professional value base and, as such, are also reflected in the core themes of this book. For example, as each chapter in the second part of the book explores practice skills, knowledge, ethics and values, you will gain an in-depth understanding of how groupworking can help vulnerable people address their needs and achieve change in their lives, thus promoting social justice and wellbeing.

Knowledge – apply knowledge of social sciences, law and social work practice theory

The first part of the book, particularly Chapters 2 and 3, provide analysis and discussion about the underpinning knowledge and theory that provides models to explain, and models on which to develop, effective groupworking practices. The contribution of theory to our understanding of the complexity of groupworking is considered through examples of particular theoretical perspectives being drawn upon throughout the chapters.

Critical reflection and analysis – apply critical reflection and analysis to inform and provide a rationale for professional decision making

The chapters in *Groupwork Practice for Social Workers* will help you to 'identify, distinguish, evaluate and integrate multiple sources of knowledge and evidence' as required by this domain of the PCF. Each chapter includes opportunities for you to develop skills in reflection and analysis through case study examples, examples from research, policy and legislation, interactive activities, reflective practice questions and annotated further reading/research.

Intervention and skills – use judgement and authority to intervene with individuals, families and communities to promote independence, provide support and prevent harm, neglect and abuse

The second part of this book focusses on social work engagement and intervention with individuals through groupwork practice. Incorporating theory and practice, Chapters 4 to 7 work through the processes and skills of planning, preparing, establishing, facilitating and ending group interventions with service users to promote desired change, independence and support.

Contexts and organisations – engage with, inform and adapt to changing contexts that shape practice. Operate effectively within own organisational frameworks and contribute to the development of services and organisations. Operate effectively within multi-agency and interprofessional settings

One of the recurrent core themes in this book is multi-agency and interprofessional working with others in groups. Also, more specifically within Chapter 2, you will learn about the different contexts of groupwork and interventions that may be undertaken through groupwork practice. Following this, the content, examples and activities in later chapters in the book, reflect the different and changing organisational contexts within which groupwork takes place.

Professional leadership – take responsibility for the professional learning and development of others through supervision, mentoring, assessing, research, teaching, leadership and management

This domain of the framework relates specifically to how you might effectively engage in the various professional mechanisms that demonstrate your work with others to support learning and development across the profession. Again, every chapter of this book is underpinned by a desire to influence professional learning, thus as you engage with the materials here you will further your understanding of how processes such as supervision, research-informed practice, teamworking, reflection and evaluation support professional learning and leadership. Chapter 8, as the concluding chapter of the book, summarises this by drawing together the core themes of the book with particular attention to how your learning can enhance your developing practice.

Health and Care Professions Council (HCPC) Standards of Proficiency for Social Workers in England

The Health and Care Professions Council are the professional body or regulator for social work in England, they keep a register of qualified social workers and they regulate and approve social work education (www.hpc-uk.org). There are three other social work regulators in the UK – the Northern Ireland Social Care Council, the Scottish Social Services Council (SSSC) and the Care Council for Wales. Essentially the standards for social work published by each of these bodies reflect similar areas to those detailed above in the Professional Capabilities Framework, although presentation and detail may vary; it is highly recommended that you refer to the requirements of the regulator in the country in which you plan to, or are, practising. The 15 Standards of Proficiency for Social Workers in England (HCPC, 2012) summarised below, relate to the standards of practice that a social worker must be able to meet from the point of registration with the Council. The principles that sit within these standards can be found throughout the chapters of this book.

Health and Care Professions Council (HCPC) Standards of Proficiency for Social Workers in England

Registrant social workers must

1. be able to practise safely and effectively within their scope of practice
2. be able to practise within the legal and ethical boundaries of their profession
3. be able to maintain fitness to practise
4. be able to practise as an autonomous professional, exercising their own professional judgement
5. be aware of the impact of culture, equality and diversity on practice
6. be able to practise in a non-discriminatory manner
7. be able to maintain confidentiality
8. be able to communicate effectively
9. be able to work appropriately with others
10. be able to maintain records appropriately
11. be able to reflect on and review practice
12. be able to assure the quality of their practice
13. understand the key concepts of the knowledge base relevant to their profession
14. be able to draw on appropriate knowledge and skills to inform practice
15. be able to establish and maintain a safe practice environment

(HCPC, 2012, www.hpc-uk.org/publications/standards/index.asp?id=569)

The approach taken across the text is also related to the academic subject benchmark statements for social work (Quality Assurance Agency 2008 www.qaa.ac.uk), which set out the nature and characteristics of social work education at Bachelor's with honours degree level.

LEARNING FEATURES

This book aims to be accessible, informative, interactive and engaging. Your learning is facilitated through the chapters by a number of learning features. Each chapter begins with a brief chapter summary which will enable you to see, very quickly, the overall content of the chapter and what you can learn by engaging with its content. The chapters also include activities with subsequent responses and comments, reflective questions, research examples, examples of groupworking practice dilemmas and case studies. These features are provided to illustrate key points, to enable you to consolidate your learning, to assist you in taking your learning further and, overall to support your professional learning and development. At the end of each chapter you will find some annotated suggestions for further reading and links to web-based resources. These resources will help you if you are interested in exploring particular issues raised in the chapter in more depth and detail. Please note, however, that Internet web addresses are current and available at the time of writing, but are always subject to updates, changing structures and addresses. Finally, although key terms and abbreviations are explained throughout the book, there is a 'glossary of terms and abbreviations' provided at the end of the book as a quick and easy lexicon for you to refer to. As a case in point, the next section of this chapter discusses the meaning of the terms 'group' and 'groupwork'.

UNDERSTANDING GROUPS AND GROUPWORK

Everyone, throughout their lives, moves in and out of different groups, as groups are central and fundamental to human activity and a core part of the human social experience. Through groups, we learn to socialise and to grow as social beings through forming and developing relationships. It is argued that

> The influence of the groups we inhabit has a great and lasting effect upon our behaviour, and also on the way we think – not to say *what* we think. (Douglas, 2000: ix)

Yet our experiences of being in groups, our understanding of what we mean by groups and the types of groups we have been members of or participated in, will differ from person to person. Further to this, the notion of groupwork in the context of social work interventions is also likely to be open to different perceptions and interpretations. Therefore, at this early stage of the book, this section of Chapter 1 introduces the notions of 'groups' and 'groupwork', exploring key aspects of these concepts and definitions.

Activity 1.1   The experience of being a group member

Think about a group that you are a member of, or have been a member of. You may, for example, think of groups related to your studies, your work or your social and leisure activities.

1. Briefly write down the purpose of the group you have thought of.
2. Think about when you first decided to, or became a member of this group – how did that happen? Write down the two main reasons you had for becoming a member.
3. Reflect on why you joined the group and your experiences as a member of this group, then make some notes under the following headings:

    i.   Strengths – What were the strengths and positives that you experienced through being a member of this group?
    ii.   Weaknesses – Were there aspects of being in this group that you found more difficult or unpleasant? Were there aspects of your experience in this group that you would wish to change?
    iii. Opportunities – What did you initially anticipate that being a member of the group could offer you? What did you gain from being a member of the group?
    iv.   Threats – Were there any risks or concerns that you had related to being a member of this group?

COMMENT

Your work on this activity is an important starting point for your learning about groupwork practice. The third part of the activity requires you to develop a SWOT (Strengths, Weaknesses, Opportunities and Threats) analysis of your groupwork experience. This model or tool of analysis originates from marketing and strategic business planning where it is used to gather and evaluate information to explore options and inform decisions. Compiling a SWOT analysis in this activity is useful as it can help you to reflect on, and make explicit, a range of factors – both internal factors (perceived strengths and weaknesses) and external factors (potential opportunities and threats) – that support and inform an evaluation of the experience. Later in this book, in Chapter 7, you will learn about evaluating groupwork practice and this tool is referred to again in that context.

Of course, we cannot comment on the specific example you have used in the activity, but at times, during your reading across the chapter of this book, we will return to this activity and reflect on your experiences, so you are encouraged to keep your notes. You may, as suggested within the activity, have thought of groups that you work and learn with as part of your studies. These groups usually have the specific function of encouraging learning together with the sharing of knowledge, furthering understanding, and the personal or professional development of the participants as their common aims.

Perhaps you thought of a group outside of your studies. A social work student, Caroline, working through Activity 1.1 above, drew on her experience of being a member of a slimming club group. She firstly wrote down that the purpose of the group was for all group members to lose weight, but then added that she believed the organisation that had set up the group also had the purpose of making a profit as everyone paid membership and weekly fees. Caroline decided to join the group because another student, a friend of hers, was a member and told her how much she enjoyed the meetings. However, Caroline had two, more personal, reasons for joining – firstly to lose weight and secondly to get advice, support and guidance on how to achieve that goal. Caroline's SWOT analysis of this experience is shown in Figure 1.1. You can compare your response to Caroline's; despite being different group experiences, can you identify any similarities?

STRENGTHS	WEAKNESSES
• Going out with my friend to the meeting • Meeting new people • Sharing menu, diet and exercise ideas • Enjoying success amongst and with others	• As a new member, I was anxious about what I should do and what would happen at the meetings • Feeling 'exposed' in front of others • It was expensive to keep going • The timing of meetings often clashed with other commitments • The meetings were held a long way from my home
OPPORTUNITIES	THREATS
• Learning new ways of doing things (new diets, recipes and ideas) • Improving my eating habits • Becoming healthier • Losing weight • Becoming a smaller clothes size • Fitting into my new jeans!	• My concern about my weight becoming 'public' • Others becoming aware of how much I weighed • I might not understand or know how to follow the dietary advice and rules • I might fail to lose any weight, or worse, I could gain weight and been seen as a failure in the group • If other students know I go to the group they might think of me as being 'fat' where they didn't have that view before

Figure 1.1   Example SWOT analysis of group membership

Although Caroline's example is specific to her experience in a slimming group, you may see some similarities to your own experiences, in particular, for example, her concerns about being a new member of the group and not understanding the rules and processes, or how she enjoyed meeting new people and sharing common issues.

You will return to considering how service users might experience working in a group later in this book, particularly in the second part of the book, Chapters 4–7. Also, as stated earlier, you will return to this activity later as you progress through the book, however, you can also draw on your reflections from this activity as you consider the next section of this chapter in which you will examine more specifically what is meant by the terms 'group' and 'groupwork'.

TERMINOLOGY AND DISCOURSE

As you worked through Activity 1.1, you may have questioned some of the terminology, for example, what did we mean by a 'group'? Or what kind of 'group' was being referred to? There are many terms used in our day-to-day language that, when given thought, are not as clear to understand as we may at first assume. There are many different types of groups, including virtual groups; in Chapter 2 you will read about some examples of different forms of groups. However, in this first chapter as a starting point for your further reading in this book, it is important to explore the key terms 'group' and 'groupwork' and what is meant or understood by these terms.

Activity 1.2   Defining groups and groupwork

Think about the term 'group' in a broad sense.

Write out your own definition of a 'group'. (The purpose of this is to capture your own ideas and understanding of what might be included or not included in this concept, so, at this point you are advised not to use dictionaries or Internet searches for this.)

Now think more specifically about working with groups in social work practice and construct a definition of 'groupwork' in the context of professional social work. (As before, draw on your own current knowledge and understanding.)

COMMENT

The notion of a 'group' may seem straightforward and incontestable. Yet, the literature shows that there are a number of ways to construct an understanding of what a group is, depending on the perspective or context in which you frame that construction. Thus you may be referring to a family group, a working group, a learning group or perhaps a social group, each being potentially described slightly differently. Here are some definitions from the literature:

> Two or more individuals who are connected to one another by and within social relationships. (Forsyth, 2010: 3)

A small number of people who have a shared identity, a shared frame of reference and shared objectives. (Elwyn et al., 2001: 4)

A collection of individuals who are interdependent with one another and who share some conception of being a unit distinguishable from other collections of individuals. (Thomas, 1967 cited in Brown, 1994: 5)

Additionally, Konopka (1963: vii), as seen in the quotation at the start of this chapter, draws on the notion of groups as ' … the basic expressions of human relationships …'. Through these quotations and our own experiences it is possible to identify four key components that make up our understanding of groups as a broad concept, as shown in Figure 1.2 below.

Thus a group is a collection of connected or interdependent individuals, usually three or more people, who through interaction and developing relationships, work towards a common purpose. All of these elements are important to consider as a social worker preparing to work with groups. Taking this further, and given the notion of a common purpose, it can be seen that groups can be mechanisms for change. Additionally, as seen in the example of Caroline and the slimming group (Figure 1.1), whilst the purpose may be 'common' or in some aspects, shared, the

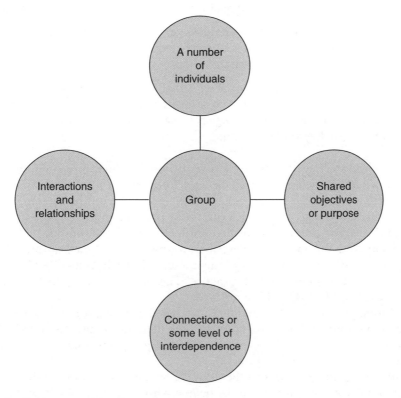

Figure 1.2   Key components of a group

individual is the focus and as such, there will be both individual and collective goals across the group. Further to this, Doel and Sawdon stress the importance of 'a sense of *belonging*' (1999: 14, emphasis in original), but also highlight that belonging arises from being distinctive about commonality and the identity of the group and its members; running parallel to this there is also a risk of being exclusive and that members become stereotyped (Doel and Sawdon 1999); indeed Caroline expresses this as a 'threat' in her SWOT analysis. Thus whilst groups are an inevitable and significant part of human development across the life cycle, their processes and constituency may be experienced as oppressive, exclusive and discriminatory (as stated earlier, you will read more about the experience of group members in later chapters). It is, therefore, crucial that as a social worker, planning, facilitating and evaluating groupwork, you develop the appropriate skills, knowledge and values to practise anti-oppressively, to understand and identify these issues, and to intervene sensitively and supportively where such concerns arise; groupwork in social work requires reflective, knowledge-based, skilled practitioners.

Here are some examples of how 'groupwork' is defined in the literature:

Social groupwork is a method of social work which helps persons to enhance their social functioning through purposeful group experiences and to cope more effectively with their personal, group, organisational and community problems. (Konopka, 1963: 15)

... that element of social work which goes on within, and through, interactional processes and structures ... which is to some degree deliberately designed and self-consciously carried out. (Davies, 1975: 7)

Social groupwork is a method of social work that aims, in an informed way, through purposeful group experiences, to help individuals and groups to meet individual and group need, and to influence and change personal, group, organisational and community problems. (Lindsay and Orton, 2011: 7)

We have deliberately cited some definitions from older literature and a more recent example. Whilst the definitions may be seen to differ, they do not conflict. Davies' (1975) definition is taken from a much longer discussion on the meaning of groupwork in different settings and as such this is one part of a more in-depth exploration, although by his own admission, the definition remains broad. Both Konopka (1963) and Lindsay and Orton (2011) describe groupwork as a method and draw out the importance of the method being 'purposeful'. Similarly Doel (2006) argues that 'purpose' is central to groupwork practice. The purposes and potential of groupwork are explored further in Chapter 2.

Thus building on our understanding of what is meant by groups and the key components of a group as shown in Figure 1.2, the definitions, and discussion above, it becomes possible to identify the core elements of groupwork that can inform a succinct definition, as shown in Figure 1.3.

Groupwork in social work can therefore be seen as the method, process, activity, or practice of working with groups of people who come together (either in person or by other means, such as virtually) in one or more sessions to facilitate a desired

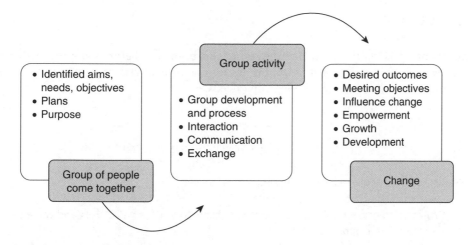

Figure 1.3 Core elements of groupwork

change, growth and/or development. This practice sits in contrast to interventions characterised by one-to-one practitioner-user sessions as seen, for example, in case-work or care-management practice, as discussed further in Chapter 2. It is important to note, too, that groupwork should not be confused with 'group care'. The term 'group care' is sometimes used to refer to residential or day services where a number of people, often with some similarities in their assessed needs, receive care and sup-port as individuals; in essence this term refers more to the environment or setting than the social work method or practice employed. These service users may also par-ticipate in groupwork, but, as indicated above, this would be separate and additional to any care and support they might be receiving in a 'group care' setting.

This book adopts these broad definitions of groups and groupwork as it considers and draws on examples of a wide range of different types of groups and groupwork practice across the spectrum of social work, service-user groups, interprofessional practice, and health and social care agencies. However, whilst acknowledging that groups can emerge informally, and that very valuable work can take place with peo-ple who come together in an unplanned, natural, loosely formed way, this book sets its focus on planned, formalised groupwork in professional practice with groups of service users who intentionally, purposefully come together.

You may also have noticed that through this discussion of key terms there has been frequent reference to the importance of interaction, communication and exchange between individual group members. Later in the book, we use the term 'group dynam-ics' and in Chapter 3 of this book you will have the opportunity to learn about how different theories explain relationship formation and social interaction in groups.

At this point, in this chapter, however, it is relevant to underline the significance of the social interaction to groupwork. Group dynamics, in its broadest sense, refers to the behaviours, social processes, relationships and attitudes that occur within and across the group.

CONCLUSION

This chapter has 'set the scene' for the rest of this book and before you progress with your learning, you will find it helpful to take some time to reflect on what you have read, and think about your own learning needs.

Activity 1.3   Planning your learning

Make notes in response to the following questions:

- Which sections or chapters of this book are likely to be of most interest and value to you at this time and in the future?
- Are there elements of the book's contents in which you already feel confident that you have the core knowledge and skills for practice? If so, which areas are these and can you identify how your knowledge and skills were gained?
- Are there elements of the book's contents in which you feel you wish to particularly focus your learning at this time? If so, which aspects of groupwork are they and how will you ensure you achieve this focus?

COMMENT

Essentially, Activity 1.3 is encouraging you to make a study plan for your own learning about groupwork in social work practice. Developing an individual learning plan can be a really effective way of increasing your awareness about your own strengths, skills and knowledge and, crucially, your learning needs and the most effective way for you to address them to ensure appropriate and proficient continuing professional development. Professional development, evaluation of practice, reflective and reflexive practice form key themes of both this book and the Professional Capabilities Framework and, as such, throughout the chapters you will be given the opportunity to reflect on your learning; then in Chapter 8, at the end of the book, this activity and your learning throughout the book will be reviewed.

This first chapter has given you a 'flavour' of the range, scope and purpose of the book, its overall structure, aims, themes and approach. You have also considered how key terms, that we may assume we have common understandings of, such as 'groups' and 'groupwork', have more complex definitions that include a number of elements even in their broadest interpretation. In the next chapter of this book you will explore the purpose, potential and limitations of groupwork as a social work intervention. Chapter 2 sets the concept of groupwork in its historical and contemporary professional context and, in doing so, it provides underpinning knowledge for the remainder of the book. We hope that you will enjoy your studies as you move through this book.

As the chapter started with the words of Konopka, so it seems appropriate to close the chapter with some key thoughts from the same author; you will learn more about Konopka's seminal writing on groupwork in Chapter 2.

Describing groupwork, Konopka writes:

1. It belongs or should belong to any work with human beings – to social work, education, psychiatry, community action and others.
2. It enhances individuals and their relationships to each other only when it is based on and carried through a philosophy of absolute respect for every person. This means honest and open with people, not a manipulation of them (Konopka, 1970: preface xviii).

Further reading

Lindsay, T. and Orton, S. (2011) *Groupwork Practice in Social Work* (2nd edn). London: SAGE, Learning Matters.
Part of the Learning Matters Transforming Social Work Practice series, this book provides an introductory overview to groupwork practice. Of particular interest with regard to the content of this chapter is the first chapter of Lindsay and Orton's (2011) text in which they consider some of the key terminology and some different forms of groups.

Doel, M. (2006) *Using Groupwork*. London: Routledge.
This book is based on Doel's research with groups. In particular, in this book, he details nine illustrative groups from that work. In the second chapter of this book, titled 'Understand', Doel explores a range of concepts that help the reader to understand different aspects of groups and groupwork.

Internet resources

The College of Social Work (www.collegeofsocialwork.org)
The College of Social Work website provides a number of interesting resources and up-to-date information for the profession. For example, there is a wealth of detail about the Professional Capabilities Framework, the domains, levels and progression across them.

2

THE CONTEXT OF GROUPWORK

Chapter summary

In this chapter you will learn about

- the development of groupwork through history
- the contemporary context of groupwork in social work practice
- the purposes and potential of groupwork as well as its limitations
- the different types of groups that social groupworkers work with
- groupworkers' roles and responsibilities

INTRODUCTION

Writing about the history of groupwork practice in social work, Papell (1997) suggests that this history is reflected in 'the essentials of the human condition – mutual aid, … relationships, helping, sharing, play and work, social concern, collective action, empowerment, survival' (p. 11). For this reason, Papell (1997) goes on to argue, it is important that we have some understanding of the background and beginnings of our professional practices. We agree with her as we feel that in order to understand contemporary practice and the current context in which it operates, we need to have an awareness of how, when and why groupwork emerged as a recognised part of professional social work practice. This chapter briefly explores social groupwork from its roots in the early 1920s in North America to the current day. You will then read about groupwork in contemporary social work practice, including the wider structural and policy context, the agency or organisational, and the professional and interprofessional contexts. With that contextual underpinning, the various purposes of groupwork become the focus; within this you will also be considering the possible limitations of groupwork practice. Having established the contexts and purpose of groupwork as a social work intervention, the final section of the chapter examines the role of the groupworker, the tasks that a groupworker may be involved in and the skills, knowledge and values necessary for effective groupwork practice.

LOOKING BACK – A HISTORICAL PERSPECTIVE

This chapter unashamedly starts by looking back at how groupwork practice in social work has developed over the last few decades. In order to give context and meaning to contemporary practice, it is necessary to gain some understanding about the past, the background to the current context and approach to groupwork practice. This quick canter through the history of groupwork in social work explores three periods of time: 1) the early formation of groupwork from the 1920s; 2) the growth of groupwork in 1950s; and 3) groupwork towards the end of the twentieth century. The next section of the chapter then follows this by discussing groupwork practice in the context of how social work is organised and practised today.

1) The early formation of groupwork from the 1920s

Groupwork is seen to have originated in the United States of America (USA) and Canada in the early twentieth century. Sullivan et al. (2009) explore the origins of groupwork in the social gospel and settlement movements in Canada and highlight its roots in religious, philanthropic and social ideals. At a similar time, the 1920s and 1930s, groupwork was emerging from communities and organisations in urban areas of the USA who were coming together to support each other at times of significant social and economic turmoil. Andrews (2001: 47) suggests that this help was focussed on 'recreation and informal education' and was more of a 'movement' than a field or a method. Thus from the time when groupwork was first being recognised, it began a tradition of being a collectivist approach to social problems.

In the USA at this time, the link between these developments and social work practice grew to the point where, by the 1940s, groupwork was established more formally as an integral part of the social work profession and, necessarily, of social work education (Davies, 1975: 15). This integration was most explicitly acknowledged when, in 1935, groupwork was identified as a field of social work at the National Conference for Social Work held in Montreal.

2) The growth of groupwork in the 1950s

Whilst the relationship between social work and groupwork became more consolidated in the USA and Canada in the 1950s and thus groupwork, as an integral element of social work practice began to grow, it was still in its infancy in the UK.

Furthermore, at this time, groupwork was only just becoming perceived as a *method* of social work (Konopka, 1963, cited in Andrews, 2001: 48) and indeed this changing perception of the practice can be seen as the early beginnings of some of the debates about the value of groupwork practice. Andrews (2001) explains that with groupwork arising from informal community settings and activities, its move into the professional sphere resulted in questions about its validity and worth, particularly in contrast to the more dominant 'casework' tradition. Davies (1975) explains that groupwork was not valued; it was seen as the poor relation and regarded as 'experimental'. However, in her pivotal report on Social Workers for the Ministry of Health in 1959, Eileen Younghusband promoted groupwork practice as an integral form of social work that would support individuals to develop in society and contribute in communities (Younghusband, 1959).

During this period there was an increase in publications of texts that explored social groupwork. One prolific author and pioneer in the advancement of groupwork internationally was the researcher and educator Gisela Konopka (1910–2003); you will have already noticed that we have cited some of her work earlier in this book. Born in Germany, Konopka was Jewish, and moved to the USA in the early 1940s to escape the holocaust. She then studied social work and developed a particular interest in youth work. She began writing and presenting her ideas and built an international reputation for her expertise. We recommend that you read more about Konopka's remarkable life, her inspiring ideas and contribution to social work. You can do this by visiting the Jewish Women's Archive historical encyclopaedia (http://jwa.org/encyclopedia/article/konopka-gisela-peiper) or reading her autobiography which is entitled *Courage and Love* (Konopka, 1988).

Figure 2.1   Gisela Konopka with her book *Courage and Love*

Institution: Rhoda Lewin (http://jwa.org/media/konopka-gisela-still-image)

3) Groupwork towards the end of the twentieth century

Literature from the 1970s provides evidence of groupwork being in the early stages of development in the United Kingdom and Europe. For example, Heap (1977: 1) states that social groupwork was 'less well developed in Europe than North America', although he concedes that there was an increasing awareness and adoption of the method. At this time, there was recognition of 'a growing interest among social workers to develop skills and initiatives in working with groups' (McCaughan, 1978b: 23). Davies (1975) predicted that social work in group situations would increase and expand in part because of the expected growth, at that time, of day centres, community centres, and more generally what he termed a 'greater community orientation' (Davies, 1975: 1). In America, in 1979, the American Association for the Advancement of social work with groups was created; it remains active today and can be visited at www..aaswg.org/.

Gitterman and Salmon (2009: xix) state that '… social groupwork, throughout its history, practice, and structure, has been an optimistic and positive way of working with people.' Thus Gitterman and Salmon can be seen to suggest that despite the changes that have taken place as groupwork has grown and developed, there may be some underpinning continuities. Activity 2.1 below encourages you to explore some of the ideological foundations of social groupwork further by drawing on an extract from a chapter by Sullivan et al. in Gitterman and Salmon's edited collection (2009).

Activity 2.1   Continuity and change

Read the following extract from a chapter on the history of groupwork in Canada,

> The spirit of the settlement and social gospel movements and early social groupwork can be seen in the ideological underpinnings and content themes of empowerment, anti-oppression, social action, mutual aid, and social justice, even though much group practice and education is problem-focused and specific to particular vulnerable and marginalized populations, often time-limited and structured in format. The settlement movement's enduring mission to provide a collective means for personal growth and development and social change toward a just society is evident in the growing phenomenon of groups that are focused on diversity and personal and community capacity-building. (Sullivan et al., 2009: 6)

- Make a note of your first thoughts when reading this extract;
- Consider the themes that are embedded in this book. In your view, how does this quotation inform current practice in relation to those themes?

COMMENT

At the start of this section of the chapter we justified the importance of under-standing the historical context of groupwork before moving forward to examine groupwork practice in contemporary social work. When we first read this extract from Sullivan et al., we were struck by how these ideological underpinnings, as they suggest, are still very much evident in groupwork practice across the United Kingdom today. We hope too, that you will see the relevance of *empowerment, anti-oppression, social action, mutual aid and social justice* to social work practice with groups as you study the chapters of this book. You may also recognise a resonance here with the Professional Capabilities Framework domain of values and ethics and the first core theme of this book, which highlights the importance of values, anti-oppressive practice and empowerment. Thus whilst there have been many changes over the decades as groupwork in social work has developed internationally, so there is evidence of underlying continuities in the underpinning value base of this work.

The chapter now moves on to become more up to date. Having read about how groupwork has developed and become embedded in social work practice over many years across the world, you will now, in the next section of the chapter, begin to consider how groupwork is placed in the context of today's social work practice.

GROUPWORK IN THE CONTEXT OF CONTEMPORARY PRACTICE

> Social work is a profession, perhaps more than any other, which is shaped by its many contexts – material, social, political, economic and cultural. (Fook, 2012: 21)

The importance of understanding context is implicitly reinforced by Fook's state-ment above, yet to do so is not straightforward as the context of social work practice at structural, national, global, political and policy levels and at the more local organisational levels, is constantly changing. Here it is only possible to give you an overview of the contextual issues as they relate to groupwork practice, but we would encourage you, as part of your studies, to explore the wider debates about the many contexts of professional social work practice by sourcing and reading the work of the authors and texts that we draw on in this section of the chapter and the further reading section at the end of the chapter.

The structural, political and policy contexts of contemporary groupwork practice

Groupwork as an intervention has been seen by some as having a low image. Preston-Shoot suggests that 'groupwork continues to occupy a variable position within social work, sometimes central, sometimes peripheral, increasingly invisible' (2007: 5). In part, this may be a consequence of the structural, political and policy contexts of social work practice and of groupwork within it. It is also important to be mindful of global influences on the profession 'as global forces shape the local while in turn being reframed in and through the local' (Dominelli, 2004: 2).

Social work practice has progressively become driven by procedural, managerialist, neo-liberal ideals which are resulting in changing boundaries and questions about professional integrity (Dominelli, 2004). In essence, the argument is that current social work practice is focussed on, and values, objective quantitative outcomes measures (such as performance indicators), which in turn lead to a functional approach to practice that devalues professional judgement, creativity and innovation. Preston-Shoot (2004: 21) even goes so far as to question whether 'groupwork can survive in a work environment where procedural practice and managerialism dominate, and in a policy context that dehumanises groups as diverse as young people, asylum seekers and adults with severe mental distress'. It is argued that therapeutic practices are being eroded as social workers are required to take the roles of gatekeepers or case managers (Doel and Sawdon, 1999).

Casework, groupwork and community work

This latter view leads to the pertinent debate between groupwork and casework, or working with groups of people as opposed to working with an individual focus. Broadly, social work practice in the current context, as described above, is considered to be individualised (Doel and Sawdon, 1999), having its focus on one-to-one relationships between worker and service user. Individual 'casework' is currently more likely to be termed and practised as 'case management' or 'care management'; these approaches may in reality be more service- than individual-led (Fook, 2012). Dominelli (2004), using the term 'casework', offers a powerful critique of this traditional, individual-focussed approach to practice, suggesting it can support unequal power relations and underplay the importance of the service user's social context. On the other hand groupwork takes place through a more shared relationship that emphasises service-user strengths. Dominelli states that

> Groupworkers have held an interesting position in social work, occupying as they do a domain that lies between work with individuals, at one end of a continuum, and with communities, at the other (2004: 84).

Interestingly however, in relation to working with communities, there is currently an overt political ambition to further community participation and empower local communities through a concept initially framed as 'the Big Society' which is now encapsulated as 'community and society' (https://www.gov.uk/government/topics/community-and-society). According to Ledwith (2011: 25) this concept is based on 'participatory democracy and community empowerment'. Similarly Dominelli (2004) explains that community work addresses the failures of casework by mobilising groups of people to

challenge structural inequalities. In part, though, these ideas reflect neo-liberal principles, claiming to reduce the role of the state and increase the role of private, voluntary
and charitable sectors (the 'mixed economy of care'), giving more choice and control to
individuals. However, at a time of global recession, austerity measures, and increasing
resource scarcity, such proposals may be nothing more than attempts at saving money
by shifting the burden of cost and responsibility to local communities. Ledwith (2011)
describes how the overall concept of empowering community-based action and control
is known to enhance wellbeing, and yet the reality of the current economic and political climate is that local community organisations are experiencing funding cuts and
closures. Citing the work of Craig (2011), Ledwith argues that 'the "Big Society" effectively labels communities as both the problem and the solution' (2011: 26). It is within
this challenging context that groupwork with community groups, such as community
development work, is set.

The professional and organisational contexts of contemporary practice

It is also important to be mindful that alongside the political and structural deter-
minants of practice, social work is also set in a professional and interprofessional
practice context. It is defined by the standards, values and ethics to which it adheres.
Therefore, for example, as discussed in Chapter 1, our practice is contextually bound
by the standards set out by the relevant professional bodies; in the United Kingdom
these are the Health and Care Professions Council (HCPC) in England, the Northern
Ireland Social Care Council, the Scottish Social Services Council (SSSC) and the
Care Council for Wales. Furthermore, you may have recognised how much of the
discussion in this section of the chapter offers useful background knowledge for
understanding the Professional Capabilities Framework domain of 'Rights, Justice
and Economic Wellbeing' in which the fundamental principles of human rights and
equality are embedded. Thus, in the same way as you considered issues of continuity
and change in Activity 2.1 earlier in the chapter, it is evident here again that amongst
so much change, there is continuity, in that the fundamental social work values
and endeavours, such as empowerment, promoting change and problem solving in
human relationships, as outlined in the International Federation of Social Workers
definition of social work (2001) provided in the next section of this chapter, continue
to inform social work and groupwork practice within it.

The structural, political and policy environment of practice directly influences
the organisational context of groupwork practice, with implications for the structure, frameworks, local policy perspectives and internal dynamics of agencies and
organisations providing social work services; this organisational context will also
have consequences for approaches to practice. Groupworkers therefore need to
understand the structure, context, processes and dynamics of the agency or organisation in which they practise, and their role within it (Alle-Corliss and Alle-Corliss,
2009; Garvin, 1997; Mulroy, 2011). As part of this, it is important to recognise that
social workers also work in and with groups of colleagues from other professional

disciplines. Thus interprofessional practice is an integral part of effective group-work practice and reflects a key theme of this book. Furthermore, the Professional Capabilities Framework domain 'Contexts and Organisations' explicitly requires social workers to 'operate effectively within own organisational frameworks and contribute to the development of services and organisations' and to 'operate effectively within multi-agency and interprofessional settings'.

Thus it can be seen that the interface between social work, the welfare state, global and local forces not only influences the context of practice, but may define more fundamentally the role and meaning of social work and more particularly groupwork within it. As a social groupworker you are encouraged to 'take an active approach in engaging with, informing and adapting to changing contexts that shape practice' (Professional Capabilities Framework domain, 'Contexts and Organisations'). Moreover, 'all of these changes ... reflect the context in which groupwork can either flourish or wither' (Doel and Sawdon, 1999: 17).

UNDERSTANDING GROUPS BY EXPLORING THEIR PURPOSE AND POTENTIAL

As you have seen in Chapter 1, groupwork is considered to be a social work intervention, but what is the purpose of that intervention and what can it achieve? In this section of the chapter you will develop your understanding of groups by considering the purpose and potential of groups in social work practice. Groupwork will be scrutinised, not only for its strengths and possibilities, but also for the potential limitations of this intervention.

The International Federation of Social Work (IFSW) provides the following definition of social work:

> The social work profession promotes social change, problem solving in human relationships and the empowerment and liberation of people to enhance well-being. Utilising theories of human behaviour and social systems, social work intervenes at the points where people interact with their environments. Principles of human rights and social justice are fundamental to social work. (International Federation of Social Workers, 2001)

The purpose of groupwork in social work can be seen to mirror this general description of social work as a profession. That is perhaps to be expected, given the broad nature of the IFSW definition, of course, but it does provide a starting point when we are thinking about the purpose and function of working with groups.

Earlier in the chapter you read about the origins of groupwork in the 1920s and 1930s. Andrews (2001: 47) states that from these early beginnings groupwork has been embedded in issues such as social responsibility, democratic ideals, social action and human connections. Andrews (2001) also frames groupwork as a *purposeful* activity that involve(s) a process that consider(s) both the individual in the group as well as the group as a whole as well as the larger community. (pp. 47–8 emphasis added)

Thus groupwork is seen as being goal directed, with clear purposes and objectives, which may be individual or collective. Within this notion of being purposeful, groups are deemed to offer 'a helping medium' (Davies, 1975: 10) with a focus on the supportive use of relationships and interactions (Davies, 1975; Heap, 1977). Preston-Shoot (2007: 27) describes the important processes of working with people and describes groupwork as 'a shared endeavour towards resolving problems or circumstances felt by the participants to be both real and urgent'. There is therefore an emphasis on the power of the shared group experience, with groupwork providing a medium for sharing thoughts, ideas, problems and activities.

At this point, however, it is important to appreciate that whilst the process of groupwork is, by definition, focussed on collective, shared approaches, each individual in the group will have different, distinct and very personal experiences, needs and desires that they bring to the group. The group or the process of the groupwork is not the end or the outcome in itself, but it is 'intended to be a *medium* through which help is offered – one means of attaining independently-stated or acknowledged goals' (Davies, 1975: 32, emphasis in original). Lindsay and Orton (2011) also drawing on the original work of Davies (1975) raise a caution that the needs of the group and its survival as a group should not take priority over the needs of individual members. Davies (1975: 55, emphasis in original) describes this as groups becoming 'extremely *group* focussed' and argues that such a development contravenes the core values and ethics of social work practice.

Types of groups according to purpose – three models of groupwork

As you have seen, there is evidence and some consensus about the general value of groupwork, but our understanding of groups can be furthered by exploring how groups are established in social work practice for a range of different purposes. Doel (2006) suggests that from different kinds of groups emerge different kinds of purpose. If you refer back to Figure 1.2 in Chapter 1, you will see what we have termed the 'core elements of groups'; arguably these core elements (a group of individuals with shared objectives and purpose, connections, interdependence, interactions and relationships) can all be seen to inform and influence the purpose of groupwork and the particular group being referred to at any time.

Whilst in any group the individuals may have multiple purposes for their engagement, here the focus is on the needs, reasons, or possible explicit purposes and goals that might be addressed through groupwork. Identifying and understanding group purpose or aims is one way in which we can classify or cluster the different types of social work groups; such classifications help us to examine, critique and understand groupwork. Thus, for example, three commonly acknowledged models that describe the purpose of social work groups are: Remedial, Reciprocal, and Social Goals models. Essentially these can be simplified as 'helping individuals', 'helping each other', and 'helping the group', which reflects how practice can influence change at different levels. Figure 2.2 below sets out the overall purpose and ideas that underpin each of these models. Northen and Kurland (2001) suggest that these factors and more are 'dynamic forces' for change. They also argue that these forces 'are not present automatically in groups but need to be fostered by the practitioner' (Northen and Kurland, 2001: 27). Later in this chapter you will read about the role of the group-worker and can then consider the relevance of Northen and Kurland's views.

Model	Purpose	Underpinning beliefs
Remedial	In remedial groups the purpose is to influence individual's behaviour or social functioning through the group process; individual social adaptation. These groups are likely to be worker-led and controlled throughout.	Remedial groups are underpinned by a belief in the value of therapy and its potential in supporting individual change, for example through rehabilitation and 'treatment'.
Reciprocal	Individuals in the group have common needs and goals and help each other through a mutual aid approach.	Essential to reciprocal groups is an underlying belief that everyone contributes to the group and brings strengths that will help themselves and others.
Social Goals	The social goals model is focussed on improving the social functioning of the individuals in the group through their interaction with the group. The purpose of these groups can also be to further social justice through the collective social action of the group. The worker is more of a facilitator working towards enabling democratic participation of all group members.	The social goals model is underpinned by assumptions about the importance of belonging meaningfully to society, social responsibility, citizenship, democratic society, social action and the collective good.

Figure 2.2

MODELS OF GROUPWORK

Remedial, Reciprocal, and Social Goals models provide one framework through which we can classify different types of groups according to their purpose in relation to social work practice. The sections below explore in more detail the differences of emphasis and philosophy, and the potential and purposes inherent in each of these models. Essentially though, in our view, these categories are not mutually exclusive, occasionally some groups may set goals that straddle more than one of these purposes.

1. Remedial

    The term remedial is commonly used in relation to correcting something and has its origins, as a word, in the notions of remedy and cure; indeed the Remedial model is also sometimes known as the Rehabilitation model. These connotations are perhaps why we feel uncomfortable with the term itself; however, the purposes of groups described by the Remedial model can be argued to be relevant to the overall aims of professional social work. The development of this model is sometimes attributed to Vinter (1967, cited in Brandler and Roman, 1999) who described such groups as being very orderly, pre-planned with a clear programme of sessions. As such the groupwork practitioner has high levels of control and power and can be seen as a significant influencer in the process. These groups require high levels of complex planning and preparation. As shown in Figure 2.2, the core purpose of such groups is to support individuals to learn, develop, change and advance their social competence through the interactions in the group. Lindsay and Orton (2011: 9) describe groups that 'offer learning opportunities', giving group members information and the chance to share knowledge and experiences. They give the examples of drug and alcohol education programmes as fitting this 'learning' approach (ibid.). Heap (1977: 3) also describes groups that 'contribute to social learning and maturation' and citing the work of Konopka, he argues that the objectives of groupwork more broadly are to enhance social functioning and to support individuals to cope with problems by exploring feelings and achieving insight.

2. Reciprocal

    The reciprocal model, as you can see in Figure 2.2, centres around the concept of mutual aid and the provision of social and emotional support; it is also sometimes known as the Contractual model. Steinberg argues that working with groups to support mutual aid is 'true groupwork' (2004: 3). Steinberg locates the origins of the concept of mutual aid back to the early 1900s (2004), although the model is often attributed to Schwartz (1971, cited in Brandler and Roman, 1999). The Reciprocal model depicts groups as democratic and reactive to emerging group issues. The mutual aid developed in these groups is described as a 'powerful helping medium' through which people help each other 'as they think things through' (Steinberg, 2004: 3). Within this there is a link to the concept of reciprocity and the notion of all group members being 'in the same boat' (Doel and Sawdon, 1999: 25) and in a position to support each other. Thus where the core purpose of the group is mutual aid, there is a sense of the interdependence of group members who have or are facing similar situations or have comparable needs. With the group giving individuals some reassurance that they are not alone, or are not the only person with that particular concern, 'every group member can be regarded as a possible resource for every other group member' (Davies, 1975: 39). In this way, the group can provide service users with the chance to gain both social and emotional support, whilst also feeling valued for the help and support they can give to other group members. Such groups can 'affirm[s] people's strengths' (Gitterman and Salmon, 2009: xiv); through a sense of belonging, individuals can become more aware of the areas of their lives that are not problematic, thereby potentially enhancing feelings of wellbeing (Doel and Sawdon, 1999). Indeed Davies (1975) highlights how being in groups replicates our ordinary lives, much as you discovered in Chapter 1 of this book, and as such there can be a reassuring comfort through shared identity and a reduced sense of isolation (Davies, 1975; Heap, 1977). Forsyth (2010) argues that a degree of cohesion is central to the functioning of any group; he suggests the need for a sense of 'we-ness'.

    In the Reciprocal model the groupworker adopts the roles of enabler, facilitator, catalyst and resource for the group. Despite the apparent difference in locus of power and control, there are some clear connections and similarities with the Remedial model in that Reciprocal groups that focus on mutual aid and reciprocity commonly centre on individual empowerment through the process of sharing and furthering confidence and understanding. Lindsay and Orton (2011) explore how empowerment can be achieved through the group members becoming aware of and understanding how the presenting issues arise from matters outside of and beyond themselves. Thus individuals' confidence and self-esteem can be enhanced by addressing the often internalised 'blame the victim' approach and raising awareness of wider contributory factors, for example social and economic factors, and 'oppressive policies, practices, behaviours and the ideas on which these are founded' (Lindsay and Orton, 2011: 8). Empowerment through groupwork of this nature can result in a service user moving from a defensive, resistant or resentful approach to services and professionals, to a more engaged and equal relationship (Davies, 1975). Issues of power and empowerment are explored further in Chapter 3.

Reciprocal groups thus have the potential to raise self-esteem and provide clarity and confidence in self-identity. Lindsay and Orton (2011: 9) describe 'groups that offer opportunities for social comparison' in that they enable the individual group members to observe others, to experience their behaviours, to listen to their views and then to reflect on how this compares with their own feelings, behaviours and thoughts; examples of groups that have mutual aid and reciprocity as their purposes include carer support groups, bereavement groups, and some parenting groups.

3. Social Goals

The Social Goals model describes groups that are the medium for collective social action, change and development. These groups aim to achieve change through their collective voice, their strength or power is in their numbers or members; the group members are the agents of change, the groupworker is a facilitator supporting and enabling the group development. The group becomes a 'place where individuals can find their voices,

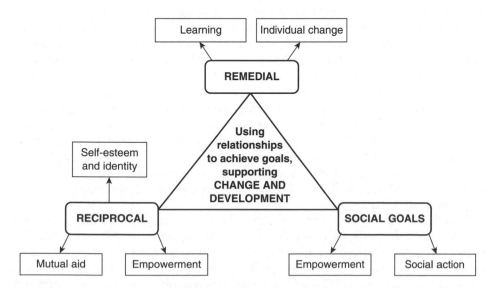

Figure 2.3

individually or together, learn together and challenge together' (Doel and Sawdon, 1999: 25). Ledwith (2011: 97) describes 'collective action for change' in the specific context of community development. Stressing the importance of understanding the different levels of need and influence that exist between the individual and the group or collective, Ledwith argues that groupwork must include an anti-discriminatory exploration of the group dynamics, issues of power, empowerment, disempowerment, difference and diversity (ibid.). Thus much like Reciprocal groups, Social Goals groups have the potential to be experienced as empowering, consciousness-raising groups and to be vehicles for challenging oppression. These models are shown in the diagram in Figure 2.3.

LIMITATIONS OF GROUPWORK

Across all of these types of groups there are potential risks and limitations for both the practitioner and the service users. For the practitioner, for example, groupwork practice is time-consuming and unpredictable, for the service or agency it can be an expensive investment in time and other resources. The groupworker needs to be skilled, confident and knowledgeable, they must undertake careful and detailed planning and preparation for each group meeting, they need to be prepared for the unexpected in relation to the group dynamics and members' responses, behaviours and reactions. 'From an economic point of view they are a relatively high-risk investment' (Doel and Sawdon, 1999: 16).

For service users, participation in groupwork holds other risks. The groups described in the models earlier sometimes identify membership through certain key characteristics which relate back to their purpose and aims. Such an approach can lead to or increase stigma, labelling and stereotyping, for example being a member of a carers' group, or a bereavement group or a mental health survivors' group. 'Social workers appreciate that, as a consequence of difference, a person's life experience may include oppression, marginalisation and alienation ...' (The College of Social Work, Professional Capabilities Framework Domain 'Diversity', Readiness for Practice Capabilities). Groupworkers need to be continually mindful that service users may already be disempowered, experience oppression and stigma and thus their participation in the group needs to not only recognise this, but also challenge and address it. A key theme throughout this book is power, values and anti-oppressive practice, but alongside this runs another key theme, the importance of the service-user experience and how they can meaningfully participate in all the processes of groupwork development. Genuine user control and participation throughout will help all participants, including the practitioners, to understand, confront and address oppression and stigma.

Groupwork can be seen, therefore, to have many strengths, purposes and possibilities that are appropriate to many areas of social work practice. However it is important to be aware of the limitations and to always ensure that groupwork is the most effective and appropriate approach to meeting the identified and expressed needs of the individuals. Doel and Sawdon raise caution about using groupwork merely as a quick and easy way to address an issue that is affecting several people, 'it is likely that if expediency is the sole justification, then the experience will be one of "work in groups" rather than groupwork' (1999: 25).

Other group characteristics, forms and structures

Throughout this book you will read about different approaches to, and forms of, groupwork; as you do so, you will gain more awareness of the diversity, extent and scope of groupwork for social work practice. You have seen in the previous section how groups can be categorised into models that help us to understand their different purposes. These models, however, are only 'part of the story'; as well as having different purposes, emphases and often different underpinning philosophies, groups also vary in many other ways. In this section of the chapter we aim to introduce you to some of those variables.

Groups of any size or purpose can be seen as social systems. You may recall from your reading of Chapter 1 that a group can be defined as 'a collection of connected or interdependent individuals, usually three or more people, who through interaction and developing relationships, work towards a common purpose' (Chapter 1, p. 15). Consider this definition alongside Payne's (2005: 144, emphasis in original) description of systems as 'entities with *boundaries* within which physical and mental energy are exchanged internally more than they are across the boundary'. The groups we work with in social work practice meet Payne's description of systems in that they are collections of individuals (*entities*) with a common purpose, goals, aims, ground rules, maybe contracts and plans (*boundaries*) who come together either in person or virtually to share, discuss, interact, negotiate, explore, develop relationships (*exchange energy within the group more than outside of the group*). Importantly systems theory tells us that systems, in this case, groups, will vary greatly, but will exhibit some common behaviours. In Chapter 3 you will learn about how systems theory can help to explain group development and group processes, particularly the common traits and behaviours of groups. Here though, we want to draw your attention to the ways in which groups differ.

Again referring to systems theory and Payne's (2005) notion of boundaries, some groups will have more permeable boundaries than others. In other words, some groups might be known as 'closed' groups, whilst others are 'open groups'. At its most straightforward, this relates to issues of membership, how exclusive the membership is, whether there are certain criteria to be met in order to join the group and whether membership is closed (i.e., no-one else can join) once the group has started, or conversely whether the group welcomes new members at any time in its existence. The concepts of 'open' and 'closed' groups may also relate to whether information, knowledge and learning move across its boundaries, in other words whether new ideas and information can be brought into the group, and whether knowledge and information generated in the group can be, or is, shared beyond the group.

Groups will also vary according to their size (the number of members) and the focus of their activities; whether their interests are individual and local, or more wide-ranging, macro, societal and political. Additionally, groups will also be formed, or come together, in different ways, for different lengths of time. Some groups will establish with a clear time limit or a planned number of meetings, other groups may be more open-ended with regards to the length of the group-life. The issue of time relates not only to the overall life of the group, but to the details of the frequency of meetings and the length of meetings. For virtual groups, using information technology as a tool to aid the groupwork process, issues of time and group-life become arguably more complex to determine. Decisions about the composition, formation and criteria for a group and its time frame will be largely determined by the purpose, underpinning philosophy and emphasis of the group, as discussed earlier, but will also be influenced by whether the group has support in terms of resources, particularly financial and practical resources.

Activity 2.2   Types of groups

Identify a particular group that groupwork practitioners may work with, this could be a group that you have experience of working with, or a group that you have read about in your studies. Then, drawing on your understanding of the different purposes, characteristics and forms of groups in social work practice, consider which of the models is most likely to apply and what the particular characteristics of that group might be. You could undertake this activity several times, applying the models and characteristics to a number of different groups. You could also discuss this activity with other practitioners, or students to explore whether there are common or varied perceptions and understandings of the purpose and characteristics of certain groups.

COMMENT

Theories and models, as you will see in Chapter 3, are useful tools to facilitate dialogue, debate and discussion about our understanding of key concepts. In this case, the three models offer a good starting point through which to explore particular types of groups. Of course, we do not know which groups you chose for this activity, however, here are some examples that students who have previously undertaken this activity chose to focus on.

- Family group conferencing – these are decision-making groups in a safeguarding context. The group membership is inclusive of parents/carers, the service user and all appropriate professionals. The family group conference is a voluntary process which is most commonly convened to facilitate dialogue and planning where there are child-welfare concerns, although similar approaches are sometimes employed to support safeguarding planning for vulnerable adults. Such groups are likely to fall into the Remedial model, being about learning and aiding members, in this case particularly the family, to become more competent and to cope effectively with problems. Membership of these groups is only open to specific people who are members of the family, or who have a clear professional responsibility in relation to the situation. The group will be time-limited and will have clear goals and objectives.

- Residential living groups – groups of people who live and receive support and care in the same environment often come together either in one group or in different sub-groups. For example, they may come together for residents' meetings; they may also come together in smaller groups for certain activities. Where the function of the whole residents' group is about sharing experiences and mutual support, it may be seen as fitting the Reciprocal model; however, often such groups are formed to provide feedback to the staff and management, with a focus on enhancing the quality of their environment and the care they receive. As such, the group may be more appropriately defined as a Social Goals model group, being a medium for change and development. Residential living groups tend to be fluid in their membership, within certain boundaries, so for example, whilst only residents could be members, this does not mean that all residents would always be active in the groups. The groups are also commonly not time-limited as their work continues and develops.

- Service user-led self-help groups – these groups, which are sometimes called peer-support groups, have emerged and are actively providing support in relation to many areas of need, including for example, breast-feeding, mental health, diabetes, personalisation and dementia. These groups are often formed by users and have a very open approach to membership. Their aims will include the provision of emotional support, sharing knowledge and information, sharing experiences and feelings, and improving self-confidence. These groups are aptly described by the Reciprocal model, but will vary in size of membership and geographical scope; however, they commonly are not time-limited, but their activities and longevity are dependent on the needs and wishes of the membership.

It may seem obvious to write this, but it also seems important to acknowledge that the purpose, aims, format and characteristics of the group will directly influence the role and actions of the groupworker. We have already, for example in Figure 2.2 and in the description of the three models, referred to the role of the groupworker across these different approaches.

Role, responsibilities and tasks undertaken by the groupworker

... 'good' does not emerge inevitably when individuals meet in a group any more than it does than [sic] when they are encountered in a one-to-one interview situation. The "good" has to be worked for, by the clients and also by the worker. (Davies, 1975: 56)

Given Davies' (1975) thoughts above and the discussion so far in this chapter about the diverse range, scope, formats and purposes of groupwork, we realised as we set about planning to write this brief overview of the role of groupworkers at the end of this chapter, that this is a daunting task! However, each of the chapters in the second part of this book focus on groupwork practice and in doing so take you through, in some detail, the expectations, tasks, responsibilities and role of the groupworker at each stage of groupwork practice. Therefore, this section is quite deliberately a broad, brief and generalised overview of the key groupworker activities, intended to act as a link between your developing understanding of the purpose of groupwork and your further reading and learning in this book.

You may have experience of working with groups in practice, and if you have read the earlier sections of this chapter and the previous chapter of this book, you will already have some knowledge and ideas about the roles and responsibilities of groupworkers. However, by working through the following activity, you will have a starting point for your learning in this section of the chapter; the rest of the section then builds on the response to this activity.

Activity 2.3   Roles and responsibilities of a groupworker

Drawing on your learning from Chapter 1 about how we might define groupwork, and the exploration of the purposes of groupwork in this chapter, draft a job description for a groupworker. Imagine that you are a service manager and you have a vacancy for a groupworker (you can be specific about the type of service, or the type of groups that need a worker if you like). You are required to draft the job description before the job can be advertised. The usual headings in a job description would be: job title, purpose of the job, specific duties and responsibilities. Sometimes the required knowledge, skills, experience are also included or are provided on a separate document.

For the purposes of this activity, focus on the following two main headings, giving bullet points under each to cover the key aspects of the job.

1. Purpose of the job
2. Specific duties and responsibilities

As you do this, or perhaps in discussion with colleagues at a later stage, you may be interested to consider the possible knowledge, skills and experience that a group-worker would need.

COMMENT

You are likely to have covered a range of points in your response to this activity and it is not our intention to provide you with an example of a job description, but to use this as a conduit for wider discussion. If you are interested, example job descriptions and actual job descriptions for different groupworker roles can be easily found on the Internet. It is likely though that a groupworker job description will, in some way cover many of the following activities and responsibilities:

- Planning, preparing, co-ordinating and organising one or more groupwork programmes;
- Locating, mobilising and/or managing resources to support groupwork;
- Working with other professionals across other agencies in an effective interprofessional way to ensure co-ordinated services and support for service users;
- Working with service users to plan groupwork, determine group and/or individual goals – within this individual assessment and intervention planning or 'contract' negotiation, may be included in the role;
- Group facilitation and/or leadership as well as supporting individuals within the group;
- Identifying and working with group dynamics;
- Reacting to and responding to issues, challenges, opportunities as they arise;
- Enhancing group autonomy whilst enabling and empowering group members;
- Monitoring and recording;
- Reviewing and evaluation with service users and in supervision.

The chapters in Part II of this book address each of these areas of practice activity sequentially. However, referring back to the three models it is clear that there will be differences in how these tasks are carried out, dependent on the purpose and characteristics of the group. McCaughan (1978a), referring to the different models of groupwork, suggests that the groupworker's style may by either directive, democratic or passive. Other writers make the distinction simply between the role being either a leadership role or a facilitative role (Elwyn et al., 2001). Lindsay and Orton (2011) then examine the facilitation role further and raise questions about facilitation styles and whether the facilitator may at times be an influencer. You may feel that this differentiation is about subtleties or fine detail, however the behaviour and approach of the groupworker is fundamental to the design, preparation, process and progress of the group and potentially therefore to the outcomes for the group and its members.

Our aim throughout this book is to put the role of groupworker into a professional context, in part through highlighting how the knowledge, skills and values are underpinned by the Professional Capabilities Framework (The College of Social Work) and the Standards of Proficiency for Social Work (HCPC).

> ... the professional group worker is expert at groupwork and the group members are experts in their own lives. (Doel and Sawdon, 1999: 14)

CONCLUSION

The aims of this second chapter were to broadly set the context, both historical and contemporary, for groupwork practice, so as to underpin your reading and learning in later chapters of this book. The chapter has covered a lot of ground in that it has not only given these contexts, but has gone further to debate the purposes and limitations of groupwork and to consider broadly the role of the groupworker within them.

Whilst you may identify a number of the book's core themes in this chapter, for us, the first theme of values, anti-oppressive practice and the use of power is most evident throughout. As you have read in the chapter, unless groupworkers understand issues of oppression and discrimination, and adopt professional anti-oppressive values, groupwork practice risks further disempowering, oppressing, and stereotyping service users, reinforcing stigma and social injustice.

Further reading

Journal *Groupwork* published by Whiting and Birch.

You are encouraged to explore the journal Groupwork, *which is a British-based journal specialising in social applications of groupwork. It has contemporary articles on all the settings in which groupwork is practised, including health, nursing, occupational therapy, staff development, mental health, counselling, child care and education, youth and community work, social work, and criminal justice. The journal therefore provides a very useful source for contemporary examples of groupwork practice.*

Steinberg, D.M. (2004) *The Mutual-aid Approach to Working with Groups: Helping People Help One Another* (2nd edn). London: Haworth Press.

Having studied this chapter, if you are particularly interested to develop your understanding of the Reciprocal model, or mutual-aid groups, you will find this text helpful. As well as exploring the theoretical basis for mutual-aid groups, the first chapter of this book is specifically about using this approach to groupwork in social work practice.

Ledwith, M. (2011) *Community Development: A Critical Approach* (2nd edn). Bristol: The Policy Press.

This book will be particularly useful for readers who are interested in groupwork relevant to community development work. With chapters and sections covering empowerment, working with community groups, collective action for change and organising for social transformation, this text will, in particular, support your learning about the social goals model of groupwork.

Internet resources

Association for Specialists in Group Work (www..asgw.org/index.htm)

According to its website, the Association for Specialists in Groupwork is a division of the American Counselling Association which is interested and specialises in groupwork. The Association publishes the Journal for Specialists in Groupwork *and offers a range of resources including groupwork skills inventories, standards and principles for best groupwork practice, and links to other potentially useful Internet sources.*

3

UNDERSTANDING
GROUPWORK

Chapter summary

In this chapter you will learn about

- theories that explain group development, behaviour and processes
  - theories that explain group development as a series of sequential stages
  - theories that explain group development as a cyclical, repetitive process
- theories that can inform practice interventions through groupwork including:
  - i.   psychodynamic theory for groupwork
  - ii. cognitive-behavioural groupwork
  - iii. humanistic groupwork
  - iv. the empowerment model

INTRODUCTION

Eileen Younghusband DBE (1902–1981) was a British woman who gained international recognition for her contributions to the development of social work and social work education in the post-Second World War period; in Chapter 2 you read about her report on Social Workers for the Ministry of Health in 1959. In this report Younghusband states that as part of establishing social work as a credible profession there is a need to undertake research into groupwork. Then in a later article in an American social work magazine, *Social Work Today*, Younghusband goes further in reinforcing the importance of the 'systematic study of small group theory and its field work application in social group work' (1973: 34, cited in Davies, 1975: 18). In more contemporary documents which set out the standards of social work practice in England, the need to gain knowledge of and apply theory to social work practice is also well embedded. For example, in the Professional Capabilities Framework (TCSW, 2012, http://www.tcsw. org.uk/pcf.aspx) the domain of knowledge requires practitioners to know and use theories and methods of social work practice, whilst the HCPC Standards of Proficiency state that social workers must 'be able to use social work methods, theories and models to achieve change and development and improve life opportunities' (HCPC, 2012: 13, http://www.hpc-uk.org/publications/standards/index.asp?id=569).

This preamble is, in part to explain the need for, and significance of, this chapter. There are a number of texts that discuss theory for social work more broadly (see for example Payne, 2005 and Beckett, 2006), all of which will, in some way, explore the concept of theory and how it informs professional practice. Here the focus is more specifically on providing a brief introductory overview and guide to your further studies of the theoretical context of groupwork practice. Thus this chapter, as the final chapter of this context-setting part of the book, briefly explores some examples of theories that might be used to aid understanding of and practice with groups in social work. The chapter is structured into two main sections, the first examines theories that explain group development, behaviours in groups and group processes, known as descriptive theories. The second section of the chapter moves on to explore theories that can inform practice interventions through groupwork, known as prescriptive theories. It is important to note at this point that the separation of descriptive and prescriptive theories in this way is a purely artificial one that aids structure and understanding throughout the chapter. In reality there is significant overlap, in that descriptive theories commonly inform prescriptive theory and thereby both are influential on groupwork practice. Finally in this introduction, we want to clarify that, as you might expect, the theories examined in this chapter are merely examples and thus we do not aim to provide a comprehensive, exhaustive list or discussion of all descriptive or prescriptive groupwork theories. Rather, this chapter offers a brief overview of a small number of theories and perspectives, selected because they hold relevance and are informative for groupwork practice in social work. We would, therefore encourage you to use the theory sub-sections in this chapter as a basis for further study, critique and analysis of the range of research and theoretical perspectives that form the knowledge base for professional social work practice with groups.

Activity 3.1   Understanding theory

Before you progress further into the chapter, undertake the following tasks:

1. What is theory? Write a short paragraph, no more than a few sentences, that succinctly define the meaning of the word 'theory'. Try to do this without searching in your books, notes or the Internet.
2. In the introduction above we refer to descriptive theories and prescriptive theories. Make some notes on what you understand to be the difference between these two groups of theories.

COMMENT

As already stated, there are a number of texts about social work theory, therefore it is not our intention here, nor is there space available in this book, to provide a detailed discussion about theory in general. However, it is important to ensure that you have an understanding of what is meant by social work theory and its purpose. According to Payne (2005: 5) 'a theory is an organised statement of ideas about the world'. Its purpose is to help us 'to describe, to explain, to predict and to control and bring about' (Howe, 1987: 12). As you work through this chapter, it would be useful to reflect on Howe's description of the purpose of theory and consider whether the theories you are learning about meet these stated purposes. With regard to the second task in Activity 3.1, which asks you to think about descriptive theories and prescriptive theories, you will be able to confirm and further your understanding by working through the two main sections of this chapter and the conclusion that follows.

Further to this, students often question how they should choose a theory, or which theory is likely to be best to draw on in the given situation, so we want to respond to these concerns before you embark on reading the rest of the chapter. It is widely acknowledged that to be effective social work practice has to be *eclectic*. This means that social workers have to understand and be able to interpret, critique and draw upon a range of perspectives, models and theories as appropriate to the circumstance. Through the processes of reflection, critique, analysis and planning, the social worker's approach to groupwork theories should be critically and purposefully selective. Thus, you should not only make sure you are knowledgeable about the different perspectives, but then, according to the context in which you practise, the needs of the group members and the objectives of the work, you should make decisions on the relevance and potential contribution of the different approaches. It is intended that the remainder of the chapter will help you to develop your practice in this way, as a critically, reflective practitioner.

THEORIES THAT EXPLAIN GROUP DEVELOPMENT, BEHAVIOURS AND PROCESSES

In this section of the chapter you will learn about theories that explain the interpersonal processes that take place as groups develop. In other words, the theories selected for inclusion here attempt to describe the processes of group development, how individual people behave and react as they come together to interact and function as a group. For this reason, these theories are known as descriptive theories in that they set out to describe what people actually do or how they behave in particular circumstances. Descriptive theories can therefore further our understanding of inter- and intra-group relations or, more broadly, group dynamics. The term 'group dynamics' is a broad term that is not specifically related to groups in social work practice. It is another way of referring to the active, fluid processes that take place in groups: how people react, interact, change and make decisions in groups, and includes the study of people's interactions in a wide range of groups, including societal-level groups; in short, group dynamics is the study of human behaviour in groups. A German psychologist, Kurt Lewin (1890–1947), is commonly credited with initiating early studies and having a significant impact on our understanding of group dynamics. You will read about Lewin's work later in this section of the chapter. (As an aside, you may be interested that Lewin is also acknowledged as the founder of action research.)

The understanding that is gained from these descriptive theories about how people might behave as they come together in groups, provides a basis not only for workers to appreciate what is happening in the groups with which they work, but also for forming ideas and developing practice with people in groups. In her work on a relational model of groupwork with women's groups in the USA, Shiller (2003) argues that:

> Having a coherent framework for group development is key for a groupworker. Without a framework within which to understand expected and normative developments in the life of a group, workers would be at a loss to choose appropriate intervention that would both support where the members are at any given period of time and help the group to move forward to accomplish the goals and tasks of the members and of the group as a whole. (Shiller, 2003: 16)

However, these descriptive theories do not, in themselves, offer models or methods for groupwork intervention; theories and models of this type are considered in the next section of this chapter. Thus, referring back to Howe's (1987: 12) ideas about the purpose of theory, these descriptive theories help us 'to describe, to explain' and potentially 'to predict', but they do not necessarily in themselves enable us 'to control and bring about'.

In the first chapter of this book, the first activity asked you to reflect on your experience of being a member of a group. In undertaking that activity you may have drawn on your experience of growing up in, and being part of, a family group or care group. Kindred and Kindred (2011) suggest that family or care groups are the first form of groups that we all belong to and as such they become the origins of group behaviour. You will find it useful to reflect on your own experiences of being a member of groups as you work through the short sub-sections that explore different theories in this chapter; as you do so, consider whether the behaviours and processes described mirror your own observations and experiences in groups.

The remainder of this section of the chapter provides an overview of theories and perspectives that describe group development, behaviour and processes. In the discussion that follows we use examples of particular theories and perspectives to develop your understanding of theories of group development; firstly exploring theories that suggest group development progresses in a staged or sequential linear way, then moving to consider where staged approaches have been developed to incorporate a more flexible or cyclical description of group development. The section then briefly examines some theories that can be seen to broadly give more emphasis to wider social influences, internal and external factors that might impact on how groups develop. As ever, whilst such categories or groupings help us to understand and differentiate between a range of ways of describing group development, they are, by their very nature, artificial in that there will always be overlaps and potential debates about which categories different theories might fall into.

Theories that could be described as staged or linear theories of group development explain the development of groups as moving through a number of, often predictable, phases or stages; such theories have gained significant credibility in social work with groups. Importantly, these theories refer to the overall development or life cycle of the group, rather than group development in each group meeting or session (Birnbaum and Cicchetti, 2005); the chapters in the next part of this book consider the detail of group sessions. There have been many writers, from a range of disciplinary areas, who have proposed different models from a staged or linear perspective. These models often set out different numbers of stages or phases, but commonly include beginning, middle and end stages, although the names for these will also differ. One such theory that is commonly referred to is Tuckman's (1965; Tuckman and Jensen, 1977) staged model of group development. Bruce Tuckman was an educational psychologist and developed the first iteration of this conceptual framework by reviewing 50 publications on the subject. At that time (1965) he identified four progressive stages, but after reviewing a further 22 studies, some 12 years later (Tuckman and Jensen, 1977), a fifth stage was added and the model now stands as described below and shown in Figure 3.1.

With the addition of the fifth stage, 'adjourning', this model can be seen as reflecting the life cycle of a group, although it remains a linear, staged model. Furthermore, it is important to be aware that Tuckman's model is generic in that it was developed to apply to all forms of groups and did not take any account of the specific context of social work with groups. This model is discussed further in Chapter 6.

Another approach, which can also be seen to be based on linear models such as Tuckman and Jensen's (1977), is Wheelan's (1990) Integrated Model of Group Development. Again this model sets out a number of stages (5), but more importantly, in later research and writing (Wheelan et al., 2003), the concept of time and group maturity is considered to be significant. So whilst Wheelan's model is not dissimilar to Tuckman's and Garland et al.'s (1965), which we discuss next, she has argued that the added dimension of time needs to be considered; in particular stating that the length of time that a group has been meeting or working together has a direct influence on members' patterns of behaviour (Wheelan et al., 2003).

Wheelan's work, like Tuckman's, refers to groups in a broad and generic sense. It is suggested that the first authors to identify and describe stages of group development in the context of social work were Garland et al. (1965) who, writing at the same

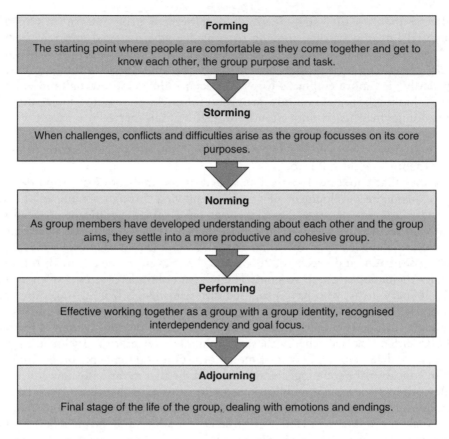

Figure 3.1   Tuckman's model

time as Tuckman produced his initial four-stage model, adopted a socio-emotional, five-stage model (Northen and Kurland, 2001). Their five stages are briefly described below:

1. *Pre-affiliation* – which refers to the time before the group comes together and the expectations, anxieties and emotions of the individuals who are preparing to join the group.
2. *Power and control* – in this second stage of group formation, Garland et al. (1965) describe how group members seek to establish relationships between each other and with the worker. This is seen to be characterised by concerns about status, influence and social hierarchy in the group. Bartolomeo suggests that this stage is 'profoundly relevant to the value of empowerment in social work practice' (2009: 104).
3. *Intimacy* – at this stage the model suggests a period of cohesion, agreement and peace, when there is a sense of equilibrium, or balance, and mutual support becomes achievable.
4. *Differentiation* – at this stage in the group's development, Garland et al. (1965) suggest that as individuals move through the intimacy stage, some may become more confident

and assertive, the groups members will recognise strengths and differences in each other and will value and draw on these; as a result different roles will emerge in the group.

5. **Separation and termination** – this final phase of Garland et al.'s (1965) model describes, as the title would suggest, the ending of a group and the emotions and behaviours that are associated with it.

If you compare Garland et al.'s (1965) model with Tuckman and Jensen's (1977) model, you will see that there are similarities. For social work specifically Garland et al.'s (1965) staged approach remains a seminal model, although there is debate about how far it is applicable to the range of groupwork in contemporary social work practice (Bartolomeo, 2009). Schiller (1997: 4) also suggests that the Garland et al. (1965) model is not 'universally applicable for all groups', for whilst Schiller (2003) is of the opinion that 'understanding stages of group development is key for working with any population' (p. 17), she writes from a feminist perspective and describes a relational model for stages of group development specifically in women's groups. Schiller argues that 'groups of women seem to move through their stages of development differently from groups of men or children' (1997: 4), which she suggests may result from women's specific needs in developing relationships.

Importantly, as the debates arising from the feminist literature demonstrate, theories of sequential staged or linear group development may provide broad descriptions of how groups form and progress, but may also be limited and should be examined, critically taking account of the specific context, membership, environment, objectives and background of the particular group. Additionally, following research with groups of workers in teams, Gersick (1988) challenges the notion that groups progress in a predictable and gradual way through stages, proposing instead that group development is characterised by 'punctuated equilibrium' (p. 9), meaning that development can be erratic and unpredictable progressing through 'alternating periods of stability and transition' (p. 38).

A further development of staged theories, that takes some account of the critiques highlighted here, are theories that describe groups as moving through a circular or spiralling (upwards) process as they develop. Again, like the staged models, these theories do not attempt to explicate what happens in group meetings or sessions, but focus on the longer-term overall group development. The theories outlined so far commonly describe a series of stages through which groups are seen to develop, these can be described as 'life cycle' models as they set out the behaviours and processes that the group may go through as it progresses through its 'life'. However, these theories are one dimensional, suggesting that groups move forwards as if on a straight, clear line. Theories of cyclical group development build on the staged approach, but suggest a more continuous, recurrent, reversible and repetitive process.

One example of a cyclical theory that is often referred to in groupwork texts is the work of Schutz (1958). Schutz, a behavioural psychologist, developed a theory of interpersonal relations known as Fundamental Interpersonal Relations Orientation (FIRO). Whilst this is a long and complex title and the theory is equally complex, what is of particular interest is that Schutz proposed three key dimensions or phases of human interaction which can support our understanding of group dynamics.

These are *inclusion, control* and *openness* (1958). Schutz's work emerges from a psychodynamic perspective, (discussed in more detail later in the chapter), as it considers how individual concerns such as needs, drives, and emotions influence human behaviour. Quite differently from the theories we have discussed so far in this chapter, these phases refer to changes in group members' self-perceptions, in other words, how individuals feel about themselves in the process. Very briefly, the *Inclusion* phase refers to how far group members feel, and want to be, connected to others, a part of the group and its work; the *Control* phase relates, as you would expect, to issues of self-determination; the *Openness* phase (sometimes referred to as the *affection* phase) reflects feelings of self-worth and willingness to participate. As can be seen, these concepts hinge on the belief that an individual's feelings about themselves have an impact on their behaviour, in this case, their behaviour in groups, and as a consequence, the overall development of the group of which they are a member. Schutz's theory of group behaviour states that as groups develop they resolve issues through these phases but may return and repeat an earlier phase if necessary, as part of the group's development. In this way this theory is not strictly linear, but explains a more unpredictable and potentially circular process of group development.

Writing at a similar time to Schutz, Bion (1961), whose work also originates from a psychodynamic perspective, is similarly credited with proposing a cyclic developmental model of groups. Taking a similar stance to Schutz, in relation to the recurrent cycles that groups develop through as they aim to resolve issues, Bion's (1961) theoretical framework describes two contrasting group attitudes, mindsets or mentalities: 'the work group' and 'the basic assumption group'. Each is characterised by its members thinking, feeling and approaching the group endeavour in certain ways. The work group mindset is where members are task-focussed and manage their feelings and relationships in a way that ensures they do not obstruct the goals of the group. The basic assumption group mindset, on the other hand, is where members' behaviours are more influenced by strong, unconscious emotions and the group can then, as a result, lose focus. Bion's (1961) framework is not linear as he states that groups can move between the two approaches, and that at times both approaches may be in play simultaneously, although one will dominate at any given time.

So far this chapter has focussed largely on exploring theories that suggest that groups develop through a number of stages or phases, either in a linear, predictable way, or in a less formulaic, more recurrent or cyclical way. We are now moving on to consider theories that give more emphasis to wider social influences, including internal and external factors that might impact on how groups develop; these theories are particularly relevant from a social work perspective.

In Chapter 2 you were introduced to systems theory which has made a well-established contribution to the social work professional knowledge base for many years. Here we consider how a systems perspective can help to explain group processes and how groups develop. You may find it helpful, at this point, to look back at Chapter 2 and any notes you took; in particular we drew on Payne's description of systems as 'entities with *boundaries* within which physical and mental energy are exchanged internally more than they are across the boundary' (2005: 144, emphasis in original).

In its broadest sense, a systems perspective explains relationships and interactions between individuals, within and across different groups to which they may have a connection, in their wider social environment. From a systems perspective, each group that you might work with is a dynamic system in itself, with boundaries. The boundaries would commonly define who is a member, who is not or who cannot be a member, thus some people are inside the system and others are outside of it. The concept of boundaries is important in systems thinking, in that a group may be seen as having closed boundaries where criteria for membership is tightly defined, or the group is not taking on members at all, or where the group is time-limited with non-negotiable rules, goals and activities. Open systems are characterised by open membership, flexible arrangements, and changing, negotiable rules, goals and activities. Importantly, those inside the system will also belong to other formal and informal systems (some open and some closed) such as a work team, their close family, their wider family, perhaps a neighbourhood community group, an educational group, a religious or church group and/or a sports team. Systems theory argues that 'each system influences all the others and is influenced by them' (Manor, 2009: 99).

Group development, from a systems perspective, occurs through the operation of some key characteristics of systems: in particular, the flow and creation of 'energy' within the system and across its boundaries; the notion of energy is broad and refers to all kinds of activity and communication within and between individuals. Systems are also considered to aim for equilibrium or balance within themselves, so that as changes occur, perhaps a change in membership or some kind of conflict occurring, other changes will take place to counter-balance the effect and restore homeostasis or equilibrium.

Understanding group development from a systems perspective enables us to take account of the individual's needs and aspirations in the context of their whole social experience and environment; so not only working with the individual, but potentially working with others that are part of their lives, thus enabling wider change. Examples of this approach can be found in family work, particularly Family Group Conferencing. Additionally, this perspective is empowering as it acknowledges that individuals, through the different systems in which they interact, can influence and change their wider social situation.

Earlier in this chapter we referred to the work of Kurt Lewin (1890–1947), a seminal theorist, with regard to early studies of group dynamics. We turn back to this theorist now to mention briefly Lewin's Field Theory (Lewin, 1947), which has some commonalities with the systems perspective; in particular it takes a holistic view of the individual group member and the group environment.

> It seems to be impossible to predict group behaviour without taking into account group goals, group standards, group values, and the way a group 'sees' its own situation and that of other groups. (Lewin, 1947: 12)

Drawing on a range of disciplines, but arguably with a largely social psychological underpinning, Lewin's Field Theory suggests that an individual's behaviour results from how they approach tensions between their self-perceptions and their perceptions of the wider social environment that they are in. The term 'field' refers to the individual's environment within which, according to Lewin, people participate in 'life-spaces' (meaning other areas of people's lives such as family, community, work etc.); from a systems perspective these are effectively other systems. With further parallels to systems theory, Lewin also considers the concept of maintenance of group equilibrium, but he does this through a complex analysis of competing forces and influences. His work on competing force fields operating in groups, for example the individual's needs, motivations and aspirations, their perception of group pressures and group needs, can be seen to have some resonance with social work's interests in empowerment, power dynamics and social justice. Further, with his focus on interdependency in groups, Lewin argues that group dynamics and processes result in the additional value of groups, essentially this means 'the whole is greater than the sum of the parts'. Leslie Button (1916–1985) later built on Lewin's work as he developed groupwork practice in the context of community development with young people.

As you come towards the end of this section of the chapter, it feels important that we should make mention of Social Learning theory. Whilst the focus here is on theories of group development and in reality social learning theory has specifically little to say on this topic, group learning is about forming connections, learning and developing through and within relationships, hence its relevance here. Emerging from cognitive behavioural theories (which are discussed in more detail later in the chapter), social learning theory (Bandura, 1977) argues that people learn from other people they are with, by watching, listening, copying and interacting with them. With groupwork in social work so often aiming to achieve learning and change, be it behavioural, practical, attitudinal or social, the ideas of social learning theory can provide a basis for understanding the change processes that can take place. A particular development of social learning theory, which is of interest in relation to group development and learning through groupwork, is Wenger's (1998) concept of Communities of Practice. This theory, with its focus on social participation as a route to learning, encompasses four key components: meaning (how we attribute meaning to our experiences, both as individuals and in groups); practice (the ways that, in groups, we express our shared understandings and perspectives); community (how we define and give value to the groups and networks that we participate in); and identity (how we create our sense of identity in our social context). Thus, Wenger would argue that Communities of Practice are an 'integral part of our daily lives' (1998: 7), being informal groupings that we are part of, either as a core member or as a more peripheral member. Participation in such groups, importantly, according to Wenger, results in learning, development and change for individuals, communities and organisations. Whilst groups in social work practice are usually more formally constructed and established, Wenger's argument that participation 'is the vehicle for the evolution of practices and the inclusion of newcomers whilst also (and through the same process) the vehicle for the development and transformation of identities' (1998: 13) would appear relevant to the values and aims of our practice.

> ## Activity 3.2
>
> To conclude and consolidate your learning from this first part of Chapter 3, summarise the points that you, having read the chapter so far, feel are key to your understanding of theories that explain group development, behaviours and processes. You should aim to have three or four bullet points that draw out the main issues, rather than attempting to summarise details of all the theories, models and perspectives mentioned.

COMMENT

It is not possible, in one short chapter, to provide a detailed exploration of all the theoretical perspectives, models and authors that contribute to our understanding of how groups develop. Thus we have provided mere snapshots, or overviews, of a range of perspectives and recommend that you draw on the sources we have referred to in order to expand and develop your knowledge further. In the activity above, however, we hope that you will have recognised that it is clearly evident that there is a broad consensus, from research with a range of different types of groups, that there are similarities and patterns of interrelationships that can be observed as groups develop. Crucially, though, researchers and authors offer different explanations of why those patterns occur, what they might 'look' like and how they are experienced. What then emerges are many different ways of conceptualising group development, behaviours in groups and the processes of group dynamics, each taking a different 'lens' or theoretical paradigm to explain the patterns observed. It is important that, as a social worker working with individuals through groupwork practice, you understand the different explanations and can harness this knowledge of group processes to support your developing practice with groups. You can also draw on your learning to help group members gain an understanding of group processes as this can empower them to develop through the processes to meet their individual and group goals.

THEORIES THAT CAN INFORM PRACTICE INTERVENTIONS THROUGH GROUPWORK

This chapter set out to develop your understanding of theoretical concepts that underpin and inform groupwork practice. Having considered, in the first part of the chapter, descriptive theories that explain group development and behaviour in groups, here we move to examine prescriptive theories that can inform groupwork practice interventions. In the context of this book, we use the term 'prescriptive theories' to refer to theories that set a direction for practice, suggesting methods and models for social work practice with people through groupwork. It is important to note however, as stated at the outset of the chapter, that in reality these descriptive and prescriptive theories do not sit in isolation from one another; your approach to working with groups will be defined by both how you and the group members understand and describe the processes and dynamics in the group and the decisions you and others make about the way you support and work with the group. Indeed some theories can be seen as both descriptive and prescriptive in that they not only describe what is going on, but also provide a model of practice to support working in the context described; systems theory, outlined in the previous part of the chapter, could be seen to do this to some extent in that it offers a way to understand how groups develop, but can also inform the ways in which you approach practice in the groupwork setting. As before, it has been necessary to be both selective and succinct in the discussion here, thus, for example, systems theory will not be revisited in this second section of the chapter; again though, you are encouraged to explore the theories further by accessing the source materials and further reading suggested.

This second section of the chapter is separated into four short sub-sections which each provide an overview of a particular theory or model for intervention in groupwork: psychodynamic theory for groupwork; cognitive-behavioural groupwork; humanist groupwork; and the empowerment model for groupwork. Our intention here is to enable you to gain a broad understanding of how each theory or model informs social work practice with groups, rather than providing an in-depth critique of the work of specific theorists or perspectives.

Psychodynamic theory for groupwork

Psychodynamic theory has been highly influential in social work over many decades and underpins many aspects of basic social work practice; it has, however, not gone unchallenged. Psychodynamic theory offers a broad perspective from which a number of more specific models and theories have been developed, e.g., attachment theory and the previously mentioned work of Bion (1961) and Schutz (1958). Developed from the work of Freud (1856–1939), the central concern for psychodynamic social work is how a person's individual internal processes, such as their emotions and needs, influence their behaviour. As such, psychodynamic approaches focus on the individual with limited consideration of their wider social environment or issues of social change. Similarly, psychodynamic work has been criticised for emanating from a biological, medical model which infers that the issue is the individual's problem, that they need some kind of therapy and that the worker has the power to cure (Payne, 2005). From a feminist perspective psychodynamic approaches have been criticised by some for reinforcing stereotypes and the oppression of women (Payne, 2005). On the other hand, psychodynamic theories have been an important element of the social work knowledge base, supporting our understanding of the potential origins of human behaviours (Payne, 2005).

The basis of psychodynamic groupwork is a belief that, following Freud's work, people have both conscious and unconscious layers of experience and functioning, and that our behaviours are strongly influenced by the unconscious mind and potential conflicts and interactions between conscious and unconscious mental and emotional processes. From this perspective, an individual's past experiences, particularly early childhood experiences, are seen as central in influencing an individual's behaviours and emotions. Also important in psychodynamic work are the concepts of transference and counter-transference. Transference refers to how previous experiences and relationships influence current behaviours and relationships, particularly the relationship between the service user and the social worker. Counter-transference relates, in a similar way, to the way in which the worker feels about, interprets and influences this relationship.

So far we have provided a brief overview of psychodynamic theory in its broadest sense, so the question remains about its relevance to social work practice with groups. Beckett (2006: 51), with reference to social work practice broadly, makes a convincing argument that 'full-scale psychodynamic psychotherapy' is neither 'feasible or appropriate' in social work, although he accepts that the underpinning ideas, which originate from this perspective, can be of value to practitioners. Similarly, but referring specifically to psychodynamic social work with groups, Tosone (2009) suggests that the psychodynamic model for groupwork has been developed and modified to be used by groupwork practitioners who are not psychoanalysts, but who use the approach where it is appropriate to the context in which they are working and the needs of the service users, thus being critical and selective as discussed earlier. Crucially, groupwork practice from this perspective commonly focusses on finding ways to support service users to explore their past experiences and to move the unconscious experiences and feelings into the conscious. Howe (2009) states that:

> Once back in the conscious mind, the patient or client can begin to work on resolving the conflict or the damaging effects of a traumatic experience. ... The more we can understand the cause of our feelings, particularly those that are disruptive, the more we can make sense of our emotional lives. Things that make sense can be controlled. To be in control of a difficult experience is empowering. (Howe, 2009: 34)

Tosone (2009: 53) refers to such work as 'symptom focused groups' or 'insight-oriented psychotherapy groups' and states that they have 'fixed membership and a leader who focusses on the individual needs and goals of each member'. The role of the groupworker, from this perspective, is to facilitate, empower, problem-solve, and to be fully aware of each member's needs, communication and development as individuals, whilst encouraging interactions and group cohesion in a safe and supportive environment. The groupworker also needs to reflect on issues of transference and counter-transference, using supervision and teamworking processes to support those reflections on practice.

Cognitive-behavioural groupwork

Cognitive-behavioural therapy (CBT) represents another wider group of approaches that has been an important influence on social work practice over many years. With roots in psychology, cognitive-behavioural therapy is, as the name suggests, derived from behavioural and cognitive-psychology alongside social learning theory. Three theoretical ideas emerge from these perspectives and underpin all CBT work:

Classical (or respondent) conditioning – is where behaviour is learnt, changed or modified through people making involuntary associations between a stimuli and a response; learning by association, but importantly this learning is not conscious or deliberate, it is passive. An example would be where someone has had the experience of eating something and suffering nausea and sickness afterwards, usually on more than one occasion, and then finding that merely the smell of that food item results in feelings of nausea.

Operant conditioning – is where behaviour is learnt, changed or modified through people making associations between their behaviour and a consequence that results from that behaviour (reinforcement or punishment). Unlike classical conditioning, operant conditioning is voluntary and requires active participation. An example would be where a teacher informs the class that pupils who complete their homework accurately will receive a sticker, or a token award, or will be allowed to leave school early the next day. The reward acts as a reinforcement of the perceived good behaviour of completing accurate homework and the pupils begin to embed this new behaviour into their usual approach to the learning.

Social learning – develops the ideas of classical and operant conditioning by including recognition of the influence of the person's thoughts and perceptions on their emotions and behaviours. This approach argues that people can learn new or different behaviours through observing others, trying out new ways of doing things, and gaining positive reinforcement as a result of the changed behaviour. Essentially, social learning theory draws attention to people's capacity to shape their behaviours, their responses and as a consequence, the course of their lives. The origin of social learning theory is commonly attributed to the psychologist Albert Bandura (b. 1925).

These ideas have led to common use, in some areas of social care, of the A-B-C model of assessing, understanding, and as a result, finding ways to support and manage challenging behaviours. This is where the Antecedent, what was happening just before the problematic behaviour or potential trigger (A), the Behaviour (B) and the Consequence of the behaviour (C) are observed and sometimes charted in order to inform assessment and intervention planning. By understanding the antecedents, the behaviour and the consequences, it becomes possible, according to cognitive-behavioural theory, to support individuals to reduce unwanted behaviours and/or develop more appropriate behaviours through, for example, changing, increasing or reducing antecedents and/or consequences.

It can be seen, therefore, that the focus of cognitive-behavioural work is the individual, their behaviours and the thought patterns that lead to those behaviours, thus, much like psychodynamic theories, cognitive-behavioural approaches can be criticised for giving limited attention to the influence of the person's wider social environment. However, unlike psychodynamic perspectives, CBT does not have concern for the person's previous experiences as it only focusses on the current behaviours and emotions.

Cognitive-behavioural groupwork is, according to Magen (2009) most commonly drawn on in remedial model groups (these are outlined in Chapter 2 of this book). Payne (2005: 136), citing the work of Fischer and Gochros (1975) and Hudson and MacDonald (1996), argues that 'behavioural approaches can be effectively used in groupwork'. He continues by explaining that 'this may be by using a conventional group as a supporter and reinforcer to individuals undertaking behavioural programmes or by undertaking interventions with several people at once in the group' (Payne 2005: 136). Further to this, citing Mattaini (1993), Payne suggests that cognitive-behavioural approaches can be valuable in community work, supporting communities to develop and achieve their desired goals. From this perspective the groupworker would start by ensuring the service users were fully involved in identifying desired behavioural changes and setting their individual goals; active and voluntary participation is crucial to effective practice with this approach. The group would then be supported and encouraged to share goals, jointly develop strategies and test out different desired behaviours.

Humanism and groupwork

Humanism can be seen to underpin the work of Konopka (1963, 1988) that we have discussed in previous chapters. More recently, Payne has written extensively about humanism and social work both as a chapter within his acclaimed general theory text *Modern Social Work Theory* (Payne, 2005) and as a full text which sets out the core principals of humanistic social work (Payne, 2011). He summarises humanism as being 'concerned with the integrity of human experience and its personal and social purposes and meaning' (Payne, 2005: 181) and as such its 'main purpose is achieving human potential and growth, rather than social change' (ibid.). With its roots in person-centred work, the values of humanism that underpin humanistic social work can be seen to be very aligned with social work's professional value base.

Extract

Humanistic Value 1: People have inherent worth and equal right to opportunity

Humanistic Value 2: People are responsible for and to one another

Humanistic Value 3: People have the right to belong to and be included in supportive systems

Humanistic Value 4: People have the right to take part and to be heard

(Continued)

(Continued)

Humanistic Value 5: People have the right to freedom of speech and freedom of expression

Humanistic Value 6: People who are different enrich one another

Humanistic Value 7: People have the right to freedom of choice

Humanistic Value 8: People have the right to question and challenge professionals in authority roles

Glassman (2009)

Activity 3.3

1. Examine the eight values of humanistic practice set out above. Compare them to the values and ethical base of social work practice as set out in the Professional Capabilities Framework for Social Workers. Make a note of where you see similarities and differences.
2. Then make some notes on how you think humanism can inform social work practice with groups.

COMMENT

Glassman (2009) argues that to undertake the processes of practice without clarity about your underpinning values is disrespectful and potentially dangerous. Thus thinking about your values and how they inform your work is fundamental to effective social work practice. Whilst the words and phrases used may differ, we would suggest that there are many commonalities between the values of humanistic practice and the values of social work practice as set out throughout the Professional Capabilities Framework (PCF). This is particularly evident, for example, in the PCF domains of 'values and ethics', 'diversity', 'human rights, justice and economic wellbeing' and 'intervention and skills'. You may find it useful to look back at the details of these domains now, focussing particularly on the level of the PCF that reflects your professional development. For the second part of this activity you may have thought back to the different types of groups set out in the previous chapter. Humanistic groupwork can be most commonly aligned with reciprocal or mutual aid groups as it has democratic and participatory values at its core. As a consequence, the groupworker takes the role of facilitator; this role is discussed in more detail in the next chapter of this book. As facilitator, one of the main aims of the humanistic groupworker is to enable meaningful, collective participation, engaging all members of the group. By empowering members, building confidence and participation in a supportive group environment, the worker aims to support individuals to express their feelings and emotions openly, developing and enabling mutual, emotionally supportive relationships.

Writing about groupwork with children from disadvantaged communities, Deasy (2011: 14) states that

> The humanistic groupwork method aims to develop and sustain a particular kind of a small face to face group that is built on selected values which link its members to each other through a distinct set of affective bonds. These affects include trust, care, respect, acceptance and anger. ... The method's objectives are designed to assist the children with their interactional and problem solving processes. Humanistic values shape children's stances and attitudes about themselves and others within the group.

The values and rights-based approach of humanistic practice outlined here resonates in many respects with the empowerment model which is discussed in the next section.

The empowerment model

The concept of empowerment and the use of power in practice is part of the first core theme running throughout this book. It is acknowledged in the literature that the term 'empowerment' is defined and understood in many different ways and that it is therefore, a contested term. A broad definition of empowerment which is useful for the purposes of this book is provided by Tew (2013: 439), 'a value of orientation towards practice – one which seeks to enable individuals, families or groups to take power for themselves and, as far as possible, assume responsibility for making their own choices, managing their own affairs and participating fully within the life of the community'.

Building on this, the empowerment model has roots in political movements and radical, critical theories about social change, supporting the development of self-directed and self-help groups. This model is also underpinned by systems thinking, discussed earlier in this chapter, in that it understands people's problems as originating from their wider, social, inter-connecting systems. It is argued that too often groupwork focusses on changing something about the service user whilst groupwork practice would, more appropriately, be founded on an understanding that the way our social structures, norms and institutions function can be the source of many people's difficulties in their lives (Mullender and Ward, 1991). Thus whilst, as noted above, the empowerment model for groupwork can be seen to reflect the philosophy and values of humanistic groupwork, with its focus on collective, mutual support, rights and democratic participation, the key difference is that the focus for the empowerment model is change at the social, rather than individual or group, level as this model 'gives more importance to the power differentials, class and oppression as aspects of society which obstruct self-actualisation and actively need to be overcome' (Payne, 2005: 301).

Beckett (2006: 34) offers this useful summary of this approach:

> The difficulties experienced by many people are the result of their oppression by society, which in turn results in making them feel powerless to influence events or to resolve things for themselves. Conventional 'help' – for example, medication prescribed by a psychiatrist – may simply confirm their powerlessness and the powerfulness of others. Real change requires that the oppressed take power for themselves or become more aware of the power which they do in fact already possess.

It should be noted, however, that authors, such as Beckett (2006) and Dominelli (2002), raise caution that empowerment can become a term that is used in a tokenistic, cosmetic or superficial way and that by doing so, practice can actually reinforce social divisions, powerlessness and oppression. Meaningful, 'power-sensitive' (Beckett, 2006: 126) practice, working within the empowerment model for groupwork, means working with a perspective that structural, societal change is needed in order to improve the circumstances of service users; such practice can be liberating, transformative and emancipatory. Thus, whilst there is 'no singular empowerment group approach' (Hudson, 2009: 48), working from this perspective requires the groupworker to fully understand the concepts of power, powerlessness and oppression, how they impact on the particular needs and wishes of the group members and how, through groupwork, these issues can be forefronted and addressed. The groupworker's role from this perspective is consciousness-raising and developing the group's confidence, which will support and enable them to actively challenge and overcome oppressive attitudes, structures, systems and services, so that they experience social justice, equity, control, partnership and transparency in making decisions about their lives. Hudson (2009: 48) suggests that the groupworker needs 'to act as a mediator between the group and society'. The approach is not one of leadership or even facilitation, but more of an equitable partnership with the group, as 'co-activists' or 'co-workers' (Hudson, 2009). You will see, therefore, how this approach links to issues of rights and how it is so often written about alongside the concepts of advocacy, self-advocacy and self-directed groupwork. Payne (2005) describes how the empowerment model has informed social and community development work and Hudson (2009: 49) argues that 'the empowerment model is relevant for any poor, oppressed, stigmatised, disenfranchised, and/or marginalised group or community, as long as members are able and willing, and need each other to do the work'.

Prescriptive theories, as shown in this second section of the chapter, offer particular perspectives on how people may develop and change through working within groups. These perspectives often have very different foci and therefore they propose different outcomes for groupwork and, accordingly, different approaches to groupwork practice. One fundamental difference, as you have learnt, is that some theories focus on supporting the individual to change their behaviour, for example cognitive-behavioural theory, whilst others focus on enabling the individual to work with others to challenge and promote change at a societal or structural level, for example the empowerment model. Furthermore, some theories suggest quite specific ways of working with people, for example psychodynamic theory and cognitive-behavioural theory, yet other approaches offer more broad, value-based descriptions of practice, for example humanistic groupwork and the empowerment model. Your choice of approach will depend on many things: individual preference based on your own underpinning values, philosophy and perspective; your organisational context, its values, perspectives and objectives; and the type, needs and objectives of the group and its members. Importantly, though, through your developing understanding of the different theoretical approaches to groupwork practice and related research, as you work with colleagues and service users, you should at all times be critical and reflective about your practice.

CONCLUSION

The topic of this chapter has been 'Understanding Groupwork', in particular it aimed to help you develop your understanding of the theoretical knowledge that informs social work practice with groups. In reality, it would be possible to write a whole book on this topic alone and therefore, it has been necessary to be brief and provide merely overviews of some of the key theories and models that are commonly drawn upon in social groupwork practice. In the first part of the chapter you learnt about descriptive theories which, as the name implies, describe how individuals behave in groups and how, as a consequence, groups develop together. The second part of the chapter then moved on to examine a small number of prescriptive theories which, through different perspectives on how people may develop and change through working within groups, suggest different ways in which the groupwork practitioner may practice.

This chapter is the last chapter in this context-setting part of the book. Our intention has been to enable you to gain a broad understanding of a range of different theories and models and how they can inform your practice when working with groups. As you move into the second part of the book, the practice-related chapters will draw on your learning about the context and knowledge base for groupwork practice. In order to further your understanding and gain a more in-depth, critical, evidence-based knowledge of specific theorists, models, perspectives or areas that are of interest to you, we recommend that you access the sources cited throughout the chapter and the further reading outlined below.

Further reading

Payne, M. (2005) *Modern Social Work Theory* (3rd edn). Basingstoke: Palgrave.
We recommend this book as a comprehensive introduction to theory for social work broadly. However, within Payne (2005) you will find a number of sections that specifically explore groupwork theory, for example within chapter 3. Additionally, there are

(Continued)

(Continued)

useful sections that explore, for example, feminist perspectives (chapter 12), empower-
ment theories (p. 247), and humanistic groupwork (p. 197), in more depth than has been
possible within this one chapter.

Trevithick, P. (2005) 'The knowledge base of groupwork and its importance within social
   work', *Groupwork*, 15 (2): 80–107.
This article provides a very readable and helpful discussion about the knowledge base of
groupwork and its importance within social work. It is particularly useful for developing
your learning from this chapter as it not only describes how theoretical knowledge for
groupwork is conceptualised, but it also explores factual knowledge and practice knowl-
edge in the context of groupwork for social work.

Mullender, A., Ward, D. and Fleming, J. (2013) *Empowerment in Action: Self-Directed*
   Groupwork. Basingstoke: Palgrave.
If the section on the empowerment model, with its brief reference to self-directed group-
work, at the end of this chapter, interests you, then we recommend you further your
learning by accessing this text. This is the latest and most contemporary text from these
authors who have previously written a number of texts on this topic. In this practical and
accessible book, the authors use practice examples and research to explore the empower-
ment model and how it applies to self-directed groupwork.

Internet resources

International Association of Social Work with Groups (http://iaswg.org/)
This American-based association has international membership and was formerly the
Association for the Advancement of Social Work with Groups (AASWG). The IASWG web-
site offers an interesting section giving standards for social work practice with groups and
a section with a range of resources and literature.

PART II

GROUPWORK PRACTICE

4

PLANNING AND PREPARATION

Chapter summary

In this chapter you will learn about

- the art of planning and preparation for groupwork
- defining the purpose and methodology of your group
- guidance on how to decide whether groupwork is the right approach
- whether the group will require a leader or facilitator
- a host of practicalities that need to be considered prior to the group commencing
- the importance of planning for endings, evaluation and recording

INTRODUCTION

The art of good groupwork is, like everything else in life, in the planning and preparation that you do prior to starting the process itself. Whilst it is tempting to rush headlong into getting your group up and running quickly, this is the time to pause, take a deep breath and put your energy into some serious planning for what is about to follow. This will help ensure that you anticipate most if not all complications and difficulties that may arise in setting up, running and eventually ending the group you are about to work with. In addition, good planning and preparation will help increase the feeling of safety in the group, aid participation and reduce the rate of drop out.

According to Benson (2010: 9), 'The importance of planning cannot be emphasized enough…' and he goes on to suggest that planning and preparation are indeed enshrined in our culture and '…the basis of many of our favourite proverbs: "Look before you leap", "A stitch in time saves nine", "Prevention is better than cure" and so on'.

With the case for planning and preparation made, let us move on to the key areas for consideration when setting up any formal group. These are:

- Purpose
- Methodology
- Leadership versus Facilitation
- Content
- Practicalities
- Referral and Recruitment
- Support
- Membership
- Contracting
- Endings
- Recording and Evaluation
- Supervision
- Self-Directed Groups

PURPOSE

In Chapter 2 it is noted that there are three commonly acknowledged models that describe the purpose of a group, namely Remedial, Reciprocal and Social Goals. Whilst it is no doubt useful to identify under which model your proposed group sits, it is far more important to ensure that the group has both a clear purpose and well-defined aims and objectives. In truth, without these the group is unlikely to function well and has little chance of meeting its goals.

The purpose of the group will often arise as a result of someone identifying that there are a group of individuals who would benefit from being brought together and according to Howe (2009: 106): 'Minds as well as bodies have a remarkable capacity to self-heal. Personal resilience can be bolstered by recognizing personal strengths, but can be enhanced by working together with others who share the same needs and experiences'. These groups may seek to:

- Address their behaviour and explore their feelings (Remedial)
- Gain social and emotional support (Reciprocal)
- Unite in order to achieve social action, change or development (Social Goals)

If you are the person who is instrumental in convening a new group then you need to have done your research in order to clarify: the particular need that requires addressing; that there is a defined group of people sharing this need; and that group-work is indeed the best method for addressing that need. Once these questions are answered you will start to have a sense of direction for the group, but it should also be remembered, as highlighted earlier in this book, that groupwork does have its limitations and is not always an appropriate intervention in every situation.

How do you know if groupwork is the right approach?

There are a number ways of being as sure as you can be that your proposed group is appropriate and fit for purpose.

The first is to share your idea for the group with a trusted friend, social work colleague or manager to see if they agree with your rationale and believe that what you are proposing is achievable. What you are seeking is constructive challenge to your idea so do not be put off simply because they fail to share your enthusiasm for the project. If they should raise genuine issues in relation to the premise for the group, then you should consider these matters carefully and discuss them with your supervisor, before detailing how you might address them.

Secondly you could consider talking to a potential member or service user about your groupwork idea to see if they think it would be something that could be beneficial to them or others in their position.

If the group proceeds, you should consider whether a service user or users will be involved in the planning, content design and delivery of the groupwork sessions. This could help to empower both the individual service user/s, but ultimately other members, to take control of the group's destiny. When involving anyone, including service users, in group design it is likely that the original aims and objectives may, through the process itself, need to be modified. In addition you have to be aware that if the service user subsequently becomes a group member, this will lead to a power imbalance with other group members (and potentially the group leader/facilitator) and will need to be recognised, acknowledged and managed appropriately; these types of interactions and group dynamics were discussed in Chapter 3 and are explored further in Chapter 6. The purpose of your group may of course be absolutely clear because it is a new group being run under an existing programme or format, in which case it should simply be a matter of reviewing that the original purpose, aims and objectives outlined for the group, still hold true.

METHODOLOGY

In planning your group it is important that you have an understanding of the methodology you intend to use to underpin your groupwork intervention when working with members, and we suggest that it may be useful for you refer back to the theories, models and concepts we discussed in Chapter 3. This may sound complicated but methodology simply refers to the model or theory that will underpin the groupwork and additionally the techniques you will use within the course of the group sessions.

Whitaker (2007: 43) suggests that '...every practitioner actually holds some form of theory, perhaps explicitly, perhaps implicitly. It is impossible to do otherwise'.

There are clearly a range of different theories that could underpin a groupwork intervention, including behavioural/cognitive, psychodynamic, systems, and humanist, and it is likely to be down to personal preference, as to which is your preferred approach, and indeed these might change depending on the type of group.

LEADERSHIP VERSUS FACILITATION

Although the words leadership and facilitation are often used as interchangeable terms, there are a number of significant differences between the two when considering them in relation to groupwork. Therefore it is important at an early stage in the planning (particularly for a formal group) to be clear as to whether there will be a designated leader or a facilitator for the group, and if sharing the role, a co-facilitator. Although for the purposes of this book we are focussing on the formal approach to groupwork, it should be acknowledged that in more informal groups it is possible and quite normal for the leadership in a group to emerge or change over a period of time.

What then are the main differences between a leader and a facilitator of a group? In order to decide which approach will best suit the group you will be leading or facilitating you need to consider the similarities and divergences of the two roles.

The leader, it can be argued, is the person that not only leads the group but is someone who has responsibility invested in the group, to a greater or lesser degree, for both the welfare of group members and the ultimate success or failure of the group process. They are usually responsible for planning the group, identifying initial aims and objectives, securing resources, setting the agenda (however loosely), identifying group methodology, leading the initial discussion and ultimately reviewing and evaluating the group itself; this usually necessitates that the leader has a high degree of control over the process. The leadership style is likely to have a significant impact on the groupwork process and the leader may need to adapt his/her approach depending upon the type of group being run.

A facilitator is someone who enables the group participants to find their own path through the groupwork process and draw their own conclusions. The facilitator should endeavour to be objective in their approach to the group, have no hidden agenda and be acutely self-aware, as the facilitator can influence consciously or unconsciously all aspects of the group process.

Whilst the leader and facilitator appear to share many common features we would maintain that the key difference between them is that the latter does not hold the same degree of responsibility for group content or process as the former. It can be argued that many of the qualities of an experienced leader or facilitator closely mirror that of a good and competent social worker and we suggest that they include:

- **Previous experience** – of running and/or being part of groups
- **Group dynamics/process** – an understanding of how they work

- **Self-awareness** – good awareness of their own behaviour and actions
- **Planning** – ability to plan and deliver the proposed group
- **Communication skills** – sound ability to communicate with others
- **Relationships** – ability to build trust with individual members/groups
- **Boundaries** – ability to establish and maintain group boundaries
- **Conflict** – manage conflict when this occurs
- **Model** – act in a way that models appropriate behaviour in and out of the group
- **Sense of humour** – as seen on all job applications, this can help!

This list is far from exhaustive but gives some indication of the wide range of attributes required by your average group leader or facilitator.

If the facilitator is working with a co-facilitator it is essential to define from the beginning the roles and responsibilities of each person; these will need to be shared with group members to ensure clarity and prevent one facilitator being played off against the other. When identifying a co-facilitator for the group you will first need to ask the important questions, namely 'can I work with this person?' and secondly, 'do we have a shared understanding about the aims and objectives of the group?' If the answer to either of these questions is 'no' then you may need to re-evaluate whether co-facilitation will be effective in the group you intend to run.

Activity 4.1

Make a list of what factors would help you decide whether your group needs a leader or a facilitator.

COMMENT

In our experience the decision about whether or not a group will require a leader or facilitator is usually determined by the aims and purpose of the group, with groups that seek to deliver a predetermined or social educational programme often needing leadership and those with a focus of mutual support/encouraging members to find their own solutions, facilitation.

As you can see we have included in the above list of leader/facilitator attributes 'previous experience' of running or being part of a group. Although we would acknowledge that it is perfectly feasible for any social worker with the appropriate organisation, communication and people skills to lead or facilitate a group, it makes sense, if you have never done so before, to enlist the help or support of a social worker or other professional who has. After you have co-facilitated your first group you will have a better understanding of not only how to plan and prepare, but also how to manage the group-work process and deal with some of the difficulties and pitfalls you may encounter in the life cycle of the group. If the aims and objectives of the group have a theme outside your expertise you can always consider utilising the skills/experience of another professional from health, probation or the police to co-lead or facilitate the group with you.

CONTENT

Whilst much of what is written above has importance when it comes to planning and preparation for a group, the content must be given sufficient priority as it is ultimately the vehicle by which you deliver (and hopefully meet) your original aims and objectives. Indeed it can be argued that there is little point in good planning and preparation for the group in all other respects, if the content delivered is subsequently inadequate or poor.

It is crucial then to understand what we mean by the term 'content' in regard to groupwork, why it is so important and how it differs from 'process'.

According to Lindsay and Orton (2011: 69):

> content refers to the what of group experience – what people are saying, what they are going to do next. Content is the substance of what is happening in the group; it is on the surface and can be seen or heard. Process, on the other hand, happens below the surface. It can rarely be seen or heard but can nevertheless, be experienced and felt.

The content of the group needs to be planned both in a general structure sense and in relation to each individual session being delivered, and in this respect there are a number of books and other materials that can assist you as the leader/facilitator in planning the content. Although we will be discussing group content in more detail later in the book, it is likely, depending on the type of group, that you will use a range of materials including:

- Exercises
- Activities
- Art Materials
- Role Play
- Discussion
- Theory
- Self Disclosure
- Guest Speakers
- Journals

It is useful to note that planning needs to be a balance between ensuring that there are enough activities to fill the planned session on the one hand, and not being so overly prescriptive that members are unable to have the space to explore their own agendas on the other.

PRACTICALITIES

There is usually a whole range of practicalities that need to be considered before you are ready to embark on running a group and these include:

Permissions

It very much depends on the type of group, as to whether you need to seek any associated permissions in order to form it. There are occasions when a group is run in work time on behalf of an employer and clearly before it commences, at the proposal stage, permissions from managers will need to have been sought and obtained. In addition, there are instances when a group will have been commissioned by others and the details of what is planned may require discussion with that person or organisation, to ensure that what is proposed is in line with their expectations. If you are running a group for children, then parental consent (or a guardian's agreement) will need to be sought for them to attend. However, let's not forget that there are of course many examples of groupwork which will be more informal in nature and the only permission required will be that of the adult attending the group (see below).

Case study

Alan is a Social Worker who works for the Local Authority, and through oversight of his own child care caseload and in discussions with colleagues, he has noted that there are a significant number of teenagers in the local area who have a substance misuse problem. Although these young people (and their families) are involved with Children's Services for a range of different reasons, he feels they would benefit from being brought together in a group to discuss their issues with drink and drug abuse; rather than being worked with on a purely individual basis. He subsequently shares his thoughts with his team manager and says that he would like to set up a group for teenagers with substance misuse difficulties. The team manager informs Alan that unfortunately the department does not have the resources to set up and run such a group, and he needs to focus on achieving the targets previously agreed on his own caseload.

Whilst disappointed with the response Alan decides to do some further research into the group and subsequently produces a short proposal paper detailing: likely costs; funding sources; a possible free venue; the aims and objectives of the group; target membership; as well as a list of benefits and risks. In addition through further discussions Alan manages to identify a worker from the Substance Misuse Team who is interested in running the group with him. After galvanising support from his colleagues with regard to the proposed group, Alan approaches his team manager for a second time and asks that he read the paper he has prepared. Just over a week later Alan is asked to meet with both his team manager and the service manager for a discussion about the groupwork proposal. Although his team manager continues to express some reservations about whether Alan has sufficient time to run the group along his existing casework responsibilities, he is given permission to proceed.

COMMENT

In the above case example you can see that Alan is convinced that his idea for a group is something that is potentially beneficial to both the individual service users and the department as a whole. He is not discouraged when initially told by his team manager that the group is not viable, but instead puts his energies into thinking creatively about the issue and producing his proposal paper for the group.

Risk assessment

Although risk assessments are now embedded in the bureaucratic infrastructure of most organisations, and this particularly applies to the worlds of education and social work in the public sector, it is nevertheless something you will need to consider when setting up your group. In some instances it will be closely aligned with 'permissions' and you will need to complete a risk assessment process, culminating in a filling out and submitting of the required form for management sign off. Whilst the authors do not necessarily welcome the 'tick box' approach to risk assessment, it is nevertheless good practice prior to the commencement of the group to consider whether there are any known or potential risks (including their significance) to you, other group members and/or group infrastructure and what actions you can take to mitigate against or remove the said risk. If there are significant risk concerns you should always talk these over with a colleague, manager or supervisor in order to make a decision as to whether they can be safely managed within the group.

Finally we would want to stress that completing a risk assessment only provides a snapshot of the risk at any given time and risk can both increase or reduce throughout the life time of the group; this is something the leader or facilitator will need to bear in mind.

Aims and objectives

A key aspect of your pre-planning will be drawing up the aims and objectives of the group. There are no hard and fast rules when it comes to this but it is suggested that you ensure that what is proposed is both realistic and achievable; with no more than three to four aims and objectives in total. An example for a parenting group for adults might be 'To improve parents' ability to understand the physical and emotional development of their children and better manage their behaviour'.

If you have service-user involvement in the planning of your group, then it will be important that they participate in helping to draw up the aims and objectives, as this will assist them to take ownership for what is delivered in the subsequent sessions. The importance of service-user involvement in the planning, delivery and evaluation of the group is one of the core themes of this book.

Open or closed group?

Before considering the size of the group it is important to decide whether your group will be open or closed in nature. If your group is 'open' it means that new members are welcome to join at any point in time or at predetermined junctures, as opposed to 'closed' where the membership is fixed for the duration of the planned sessions. The decision as to whether it should be an open or closed group is likely to depend on the type of group being run. If for instance the group is informal in nature and provides a vehicle for mutual support, it may be possible to run this on an open group basis, whereas when a prescribed programme is being delivered and/or there is a high requirement for trust/confidentiality, a closed group may be more appropriate.

Group size and mix

When planning you will need to carefully consider how many members will be invited to join your group, as well as the minimum and maximum numbers to enable the group to function well. Although you may be able to manage a larger number in the group if you are running it with a co-facilitator, there are a range of practicalities you will need to consider, including the size of the venue, the nature of the sessions, and the optimum size of any group. It is suggested by Vernelle (1994: 8) that 'most groups work better and feel more friendly if they do not exceed a dozen'. The authors tend to agree and have found in their experience that around 8–10 people is a good group size, where members do not have to overly compete to be heard within sessions.

The mix of your group in gender terms is, on occasions, self selecting due to the purpose or type of group being run, for instance in a group for adolescent girls aimed at preventing teenage pregnancy. However for most other groups you will not be concerned about the membership mix in terms of gender, ethnicity, culture, race, disability, sexuality or religious background, unless this leads to an obvious imbalance or poses a significant difficulty with regard to group process.

Venue

If you have ever been to a training session and been asked to fill out an evaluation form, one of the issues that you may often be invited to comment on, in addition to the food at lunch, is the suitability of the venue. Therefore when running a group it is really important that you choose the most appropriate setting for the task in hand. What then do you need to bear in mind when choosing the venue for your group?

Firstly, the venue needs to be appropriate for the purpose and you need to have considered the following:

- Size – Will the venue comfortably accommodate the number of people attending the group?
- Cost – Is the cost a factor in deciding the ultimate venue?
- Suitability – Depending on the type of group being run, will it provide a confidential setting or 'safe space' for members and be free from interruptions and/or noise? Will it provide the necessary toilet and other facilities, for example a kitchen to make a drink during any planned break?
- Access – Physical access will be required at the group venue in terms of wheelchair ramps, lifts, etc.

- Availability – Is the venue consistently available at the right time of the day/night for the duration of the group?
- Location – Is the venue situated in the right geographical area, close to where the members reside?
- Symbolism – Consider whether the venue for the group (if it were based for instance, in a religious building or a local authority setting) could act as a deterrent to potential members.

Although all of the above are important and will need to be reflected upon carefully, the ultimate choice of venue is often based on finding the best compromise of the above factors.

Transport

Whilst it is hopefully the case that the venue for the group will be within easy access of all potential members, the leader or facilitator will nevertheless have to consider whether they are open or indeed able, to provide/fund transport for anyone who may be precluded from attending otherwise. It should be recognised that there is a potential danger in providing transport for some members and not for others, as this may lead to a power imbalance in the group and/or lead to feelings of resentment.

Length of sessions/frequency

In the course of planning the process there will need to be thought given to the number of sessions over which the group will run, the duration of each session and the frequency that the group will meet. Once again there are no hard and fast rules but it is common for the life of a group to be somewhere between 6–12 sessions, whilst acknowledging that some groups will not have any fixed duration. The type of group, the material used and issues to be covered will, by and large, dictate these matters.

Resources

The best group leaders and facilitators will, in the course of their planning and preparation, take account of what materials and equipment (including cost) they will need in the course of the forthcoming groupwork sessions. Once obtained the leader/facilitator will need to be clear about where such group materials and equipment will be stored and ensure that this arrangement will provide a secure place for them and any necessary confidentiality required.

Funding

Whilst it is important to have researched and planned the above aspects of the group in order to provide clarity about the likely funding required, the leader or facilitator will need to know that such funds are available. There are occasions when groups can be run at little or no cost, whereas others will require a funding commitment for the cost of venue, required activities, transport and materials/equipment. However, it is a good use of your time at an early stage in planning and development of any group to identify potential sources of funding and sound out whether these will be available to you before progressing further.

Confidentiality

It is important to be aware that some group members may not want the fact that they are attending the group to be disclosed to anyone outside. Consequently maintaining a high degree of confidentiality around group membership, and indeed content, will be key to maintaining their engagement and attendance at the group. The significance of establishing clarity around group boundaries, including confidentiality, is dealt with in much more depth in Chapter 5.

Child care arrangements

Another consideration with particular types of groups will be whether to offer child care to members, which will help encourage their attendance and engagement with the process. This will obviously need costing and have to be offered in a way that is compliant with child care legislation and regulations.

Contract

The issue of contracting is considered later in Chapter 5, but will need to be borne in mind by the leader or facilitator and relates to how group members will be engaged in the process prior to the commencement of the groupwork sessions. This may need those running the group to meet up with potential members before the process begins in order to explain the purpose and structure of the group, the proposed content and get them to sign some form of written contract.

Communication

This is an area that is often overlooked at your peril, as establishing clarity around channels of communication saves time and energy further down the line. It is vital that you are clear in your expectations about how you as leader/facilitator will communicate with group members prior to, during and indeed after the groupwork sessions have finished. There is equally a need for a statement of expectation about all communication between members outside the group, to avoid subsequent misunderstandings.

Anti-discriminatory and anti-oppressive practice

In setting up any group you will need to ensure that as leader or facilitator you are aware of the concepts of anti-discriminatory and anti-oppressive practice.

When considering the concept of anti-discriminatory practice Okitikpi and Aymer (2010: 9–10) suggest that the starting point is for the practitioner firstly to acknowledge the existence of discrimination in society, as this demonstrates an ability to be open and 'look beyond our own experiences'. In discussing what is meant by the concept they refer to Payne (2005: 10) who highlights that 'discrimination means identifying individuals and groups with certain characteristics and treating them less well than people or groups with conventionally valued characteristics'; and could be on the basis of age, gender, race, ethnicity, culture, disability, sexuality, etc. It is therefore important that you are able to recognise, as the leader or facilitator, the vulnerability of some members/service users within the group and ensure that your actions do not reinforce discrimination or perpetuate oppression towards them.

According to Doel and Sawdon (1999: 52), 'Groups are microcosms of the wider society, capable of amplifying and reinforcing oppression as well as challenging it'.

Whilst you cannot necessarily plan for your group to operate in an anti-oppressive way, you can ensure that you are aware of the possibility of oppression occurring and guard against it. In order to achieve this we firstly need to define what we mean by the word 'oppression' and understand the different forms it may take when considering groupwork.

1. The word oppress is defined by the Concise Oxford English Dictionary (2011: 1004) as meaning:

    'keep in subjection and hardship' or to 'make distressed or anxious'

As a leader or facilitator you will need to be aware that you may have members that have felt oppressed in their 'everyday life' before joining the group. In addition there may be a number of individuals who feel that they are experiencing oppression as a direct result of being compelled to attend the group, perhaps because they have to do so as a requirement of a legal order, an agency expectation of them or due to it being an educational component of their course. Finally, there is the possibility that during the life of the group, individual members may feel that they have a lack of power and are disempowered by the actions/behaviour of the leader, facilitator or other members.

What then can the leader/facilitator do to mitigate the incidence of discrimination and oppression taking place within the group? Whilst there is no specific way to prevent individual members feeling disempowered and oppressed, it is suggested that the following actions may help to diminish the possibility of this occurring:

- Service User/Member involvement in the planning and/or delivery of the group sessions
- Supervision for leader or facilitator to help increase their self-awareness
- Clarification of roles and responsibilities of all those attending the group including the leader, facilitator and members

- The creation of an open and trusting group environment where members are encouraged to question or raise issues, and feel they are being heard
- The leader or facilitator to address and challenge oppression within the group when it occurs; and also encourages others to do so
- Sessions to include an opportunity for feedback on the content/process and evidence that this has an influence on subsequent group sessions
- Develop a system of evaluation and feedback at the conclusion of the group

Information technology

Finally you will need to make a decision about whether you intend to use information technology (IT) as part of the groupwork sessions you are planning. There are a range of roles that IT can usefully play within a group session, but caution is needed to ensure that it is used thoughtfully to enhance the issue under discussion, rather than just for its own sake; and you may legitimately decide not to use IT at all. The ways in which the leader or facilitator could use IT are no doubt endless, but some examples include:

- Video – the filming and playing back of a specific role play or exercise
- Interactive whiteboard – for Leader/Facilitator/Members to illustrate or record information within the sessions
- Overhead projector/screen – to show documentaries or film clips to reinforce particular issues
- Internet – using the Internet to access video clips, etc.

It is also possible to utilise the world of social media in terms of sites like Facebook, Twitter, etc., in order to impart information and set up discussions with members between group sessions. However you will need to ensure that if you use any form of technology you do not inadvertently exclude anyone who does not, for instance, have access to a computer or who is perhaps unable to access one because of their disability.

The only other warning that needs to be given in relation to IT is that you need to take time in the preparation stage to familiarise yourself with the technology you are proposing to use, as there is nothing worse than when it fails to operate and you are left floundering. The authors' tip is to make sure that you always have some form of backup, in terms of printed material or another exercise you can move on to if your IT doesn't work for some reason.

REFERRAL AND RECRUITMENT

The next stage in the planning is to map out your strategy around the process for referral and recruitment to the group. The method of referral to the group will depend on a range of factors, including the type of group you are running, but largely falls into the following four categories:

- Self-Referral – the potential member opts to join the group
- Invitation – the member is invited to attend the group by the leader or facilitator
- Agency Nomination – an agency or organisation nominates the member (with their agreement) to attend the group
- Compulsion – the member will attend the group as a requirement of a legal order, an agency expectation of them, or due to it being an educational component of their course

There will be some occasions when the referral process is a combination of one or more of these categories. However, the leader/facilitator will need to be aware of the fact that the route that someone takes into the group can have a significant impact on their ability to connect and engage with the subsequent group processes. A clear example of this is when group members have to attend the group as a result of a legal order or some form of requirement on them and this can lead to what we term 'reluctant members'. It is often the case that 'reluctant members' resent having to attend the group and can on occasions act this out through the display of passive, aggressive or indeed compliant behaviours – all of which can be disruptive in their own way; and indeed are not unique solely to 'reluctant members'.

In order to capture the information you need, in relation to potential members, it is useful to devise a short written referral form. This can assist you in gathering the usual sort of administration and health and safety information that relates to each potential member's name, address, date of birth, contact number, etc., and can prove useful if the group were to become oversubscribed and there was a need to prioritise referrals. It is suggested that any referral form should reiterate the criteria (if any) for attending the group to assist potential group members or those nominating them, when filling in the referral.

The way in which you advertise your group will again be dependent on the type of group that is being run, but unless the group is informal or self-selecting it likely that it will need some form of publicity to promote it. In our experience there are certain things that you need to bear in mind when publishing a group, in order to ensure that you target the right people and these include:

- **Timing** – publicise the group at least 6–8 weeks before the planned start date
- **Wording** – ensure your flyer/advertisement uses clear and simple language and decide whether the publicity will be in English only or also translated into other languages (if you do so, you will need to ensure that you can offer the necessary translation/interpreting services within the group)
- **Criteria** – make certain you have clearly defined criteria for the group, including whether attendance is voluntary or mandatory
- **Publicity** – decide where to publicise/advertise the group in terms of using word of mouth, likely places for flyers, publications that can be utilised and agencies/organisations that will assist in promoting the group or provide it with nominations

In addition to the above it is worth the leader or facilitator focussing their recruitment efforts on making contact with any known potential members and by encouraging appropriate professionals in the community to make nominations for the group.

It is important that the above publicity then subsequently turns into referrals for the forthcoming group and ultimately these translate into actual attending group members. Once the referrals are received you will need to ensure that you have allowed sufficient time, prior to the commencement of the group, to visit members or make contact with them, in order to explain how the group will run and answer any questions they may have. However, you will need to bear in mind that it is not unusual to find that only about two-thirds of those who have stated they will attend the group actually turn up to the first session (and therefore you will need to allow for this when planning for the group).

SUPPORT

In the process of recruiting members for the group you will hopefully have the opportunity to meet with them to talk about their previous experiences of groups, whether positive or negative, and ascertain whether they require any specific support (due to disability or other reasons), before, during or after the group sessions. In addition, as the leader or facilitator you will be able to discuss with the member what form the sessions will take and be able to ascertain if they are likely to have any difficulties with what is being proposed. On other occasions the issue of support that an individual member may require may not become apparent until they actually attend the first group session and you are made aware, by their behaviour or comments, that they are not coping or comfortable in the setting. If this is the case you will need to speak to them on a one-to-one basis prior to the next group session to ascertain how you can best support them through the process.

In a more general sense the leader/facilitator should always seek to tailor the materials/exercises being used during sessions to the age, understanding and ability of those members attending the group.

There is then the support that may be needed to assist the service user/potential member to participate in the planning and/or delivery of the group itself. This is likely to involve you as the leader/facilitator in initially meeting up with the service user to explain the proposed aims and objectives of the group and seek their involvement in the project. In order to ensure that the service user's involvement and participation in the process is not just tokenistic you will need to consider with them how they can best be supported, including: holding future planning sessions at an appropriate time and venue that suits the service user; meeting any reasonable costs incurred by them as a result of their involvement in the process; and ensuring that they receive all relevant paper work.

MEMBERSHIP

When it comes to the membership of your group you may feel that this is out of your direct control and whilst to some degree this is true, there are a range of factors over which you can have influence. At the recruitment stage the leader or facilitator should reflect on the following issues that will ultimately shape your subsequent membership:

- **Numbers** – depending on the type of group, it is important that a view is taken about the minimum and maximum members required for the group to function effectively. As highlighted previously this may be proscribed by a number of factors including the size of the venue and indeed the purpose of the group itself.
- **Gender** – there are occasions where the aims and objectives of the group or the subject matter dictate that members should be of a single sex, for example, a women's breast cancer support group. On other occasions your only concern gender wise will be considering whether there are any benefits in regard to group function with having a gender balance, or whether this is simply not relevant.
- **Age** – there should be no reason to exclude or discriminate against potential members purely on the grounds of age. Whilst this should be adhered to as a general principle, the overriding factor must be selecting members based on the purpose of the group and sometimes this will mean that it is age specific (like a support group for young carers), and should be clearly identified within the referral criteria.
- **Ethnicity/race/culture** – in a similar way to Gender and Age there will be occasions when the subject matter leads to the group containing people from a specific ethnic background, race or culture, such as with a group for Black African young men seeking asylum in the UK. However, on most occasions the makeup of the group in terms of ethnicity, race and culture will not be something of particular concern to you as the leader or facilitator, other than maintaining a cultural awareness in terms of group membership.
- **Religious views and/or beliefs** – other than groups set up to support people from a specific faith or designated belief, it is unlikely that religious views and/or beliefs will be directly relevant to you in terms of preparing for your group.
- **Sexual orientation** – as with Ethnicity/Race/Culture above, unless the focus of your group is directly related to sexuality then the sexual orientation of members is unlikely to be relevant to you in the group planning process.
- **Extreme views and opinions** – in the process of recruiting members for the group it is possible that a potential member will disclose a view or opinion that is likely to cause significant offence or insult to others in the group. If this is obvious to you as the leader/facilitator you will need to take a view about whether it is still conducive to include this member in the group. Whilst you should be careful not to exclude a potential member just because it may be difficult to have them in the group, you do need to balance this against the impact their presence may have on others and the subsequent functioning of the group.

The above, which is not by any means a comprehensive list, is a quick way of profiling group membership and ensuring that you are aware of any potential issues or difficulties that may arise when the group begins. If you are unsure of how to address concerns about membership, then you should discuss these with your supervisor, co-facilitator and/or other trusted colleague/friend (whilst maintaining confidentiality).

Case study

Shirley is a social worker who is employed by a hospice specialising in adult care, which is funded predominantly through charitable donations. Following the death of several women on the unit, their male partners had expressed an interest to Shirley in being part of a support group. After some deliberation a decision was made that the best approach would be to make the group time-limited and have a semi-structured approach. The eight individuals considered for the group were all men whose wives had died in the last six months. However during the planning process Shirley was approached by another man who felt that he may also benefit from the proposed group. The only discernible difference between this man and the other group members, was the fact that he had had a male, rather than a female partner who had died. Consequently, Shirley had to decide whether it was appropriate for the new member to simply join the identified group and if this happened what consequences, if any, there may be.

COMMENT

It may appear on first reading that all nine men have had a common experience, resulting from the death of a partner that could unite them. However it is important to consider difference and in this scenario one of the members has had a male partner die, whilst the others have had female partners who have died. Therefore there are potentially subtle and possibly significant differences in their experiences and/or attitudes towards the death of their partner, which needs to carefully considered if bringing them together in a group setting.

CONTRACTING

Prior to members attending the group it is good practice, as stated previously, for the leader or facilitator to meet or make contact with them, in order to begin the contracting process. This is the first opportunity to ensure that the potential member understands: the purpose of the group; how many sessions it will be run over; details of the venue, dates and timing; and the content of the sessions – and this also allows them an opportunity to ask any questions they may have.

At the initial group session the leader or facilitator will need to work with the group to produce a contract, and a decision will need to be made at the initial planning stage as to whether this will be a verbal or written contract. It is also important to decide whether the 'ground rules' and 'expectations' for the group will be drawn up by the leader/facilitator in advance and then simply shared with the group at the initial session, or whether (as is more usual) members will be actively encouraged to contribute to this process.

Doel and Sawdon (1999: 123) maintain that the latter 'offers a unique opportunity for members to develop their own explicit protocol, agreed and negotiated and capable of being changed, an active process which is likely to be a contrast to the passive, "implicit" absorption of family and social conventions'.

The ground rules and expectations are part of the boundary setting for the group and will need to detail the behaviour expected from the leader/facilitator and members, both during sessions and throughout the duration of the group. It will also need to set out sanctions, stating what will happen if rules are broken; including whether members can be excluded from the group. A key imperative will be establishing the ground rules around confidentiality, as members will need to feel safe within the group and know that information shared by them will be protected. The issue of confidentiality will be returned to in more detail in later chapters.

Case study

Helen is a Family Placement Social Worker working for an Independent Foster Agency and is in the process of setting up mandatory support group sessions for a number of identified foster carers. The support group is something that a number of the foster carers have asked the agency to provide and all those due to attend are already aware of the arrangements and have committed to attend all six sessions. With just two weeks before the group commences Helen is making her planned pre-group visits to complete the contracting process with each foster carer. When visiting a foster carer called Megan, Helen is told by her that she is now only prepared to attend the group if another foster carer, who she has recently fallen out with, is excluded from the group.

COMMENT

Helen is faced with a dilemma as Megan, who had previously agreed to attend the group, wants to try and renegotiate the basis of her attendance at this final contracting session. This is also potentially a challenge to Helen's leadership of the group, for if she agrees to Megan's terms for her attendance and excludes the other foster carer, any authority (perceived or otherwise) may well be undermined if this is disclosed to other members. As this is a mandatory group for the foster carers, Megan is expected to attend and Helen could simply try to insist that she does so, by exerting her authority as the foster carer's employer. However, if she does and both foster carers are in the group this could have a serious impact on both group dynamics and process. In the end she decides to get Megan and the other foster carer together and through discussion of the issues, manages to resolve the conflict between them, and they subsequently both attend the group.

ENDINGS

It may seem strange to consider 'endings' when you are still at the point of planning your group, but they are extremely important and preparation for them is crucial. The reason you should plan for 'endings' is because they provide group members with the opportunity to disengage from the group process in a positive way, perform closing rituals, and say goodbye to the leader/facilitator and other members, remembering any members that have already left the group or failed to attend the last session.

In addition endings provide the space for members to reflect upon what they as individuals have achieved over the life of the group and time needs to be set aside in the group programme to allow this to happen. As part of planning the leader or facilitator will need to ensure that they raise the issue of 'endings' with the group at an early stage in its development to allow members time to contemplate (and indeed contribute to) how they wish this process to happen.

RECORDING AND EVALUATION

There are certain administration tasks that need to be considered by the leader or facilitator at the planning stage in relation to what you will record of the group process and what evaluation will be carried out in relation to the group itself.

The recording of the group is likely to take one of two forms, namely writing up exercises or activities recorded during the group session and/or an analytical summary of the group content/process after each session. If the group has been commissioned by an agency or organisation you will obviously need to check whether they have a proscribed format with regard to the process of recording. It will also need to be decided by the leader or facilitator what part of the recording, if any, will be shared with the group.

An evaluation of the group is important and the leader or facilitator will need to decide whether it should conducted at both a mid-way point and the conclusion of the group, or just the latter. When held at the end of the group, will the evaluation be part of the final session or subsequently sent out to members in a written form for them to complete and return? A verbal evaluation could also be undertaken as an alternative. Whatever the case an evaluation is likely to support those running the group to gain a better understanding of the following issues:

- Members' views of administration processes/joining instructions
- What members felt was positive/negative about the sessions
- How the group sessions or process could be improved
- Whether the aims and objectives of the group have been achieved
- Feedback on the effectiveness of the leader/facilitator

Furthermore the evaluation should help provide information to the leader/facilitator about the group in general, assist with feeding back to commissioners and inform the design of any future groups.

Activity 4.2

Design a simple group session record in order to document the content and process of what had occurred in a particular groupwork session. Think carefully about the sorts of areas you may want to record information about and how this form may help you in feeding back to members and writing any end of group reports.

COMMENT

We will come back to consider recording and evaluation in more depth in the course of Chapter 7, when we will look at the group session record you have designed.

SUPERVISION

Prior to the group commencing it will be necessary to identify someone to provide you, as leader or facilitator, with supervision and support during the lifetime of the group. The involvement of the supervisor should ideally commence at the group planning stage and it is recommended that this person is not your line manager (if running a group in a work place setting) as this can lead to subsequent difficulties in terms of whether your ultimate accountability is to the organisation or the members of the group. In contrast, an external supervisor can provide support without the shackles of responsibility to any particular employer or organisation and this may prove a more objective resource under the circumstances. The other question that will need to be considered is whether, if you are working with a co-facilitator, you should receive joint supervision from a single supervisor or have separate supervisors for each of you; there are clearly pros and cons to both options.

   The supervisor is there to assist the leader/facilitator to disentangle the group issues from those of their own. They are there to help you make sense of the group dynamics that are in play and identify where the power (and perceived power) sits at any given time. A supervisor can help you reflect on behaviour and attitudes demonstrated within group sessions and how you may be able to manage, address or respond to these situations, as well as being aware of conscious and unconscious processes taking place within the group. As a leader, your supervisor will help you consider your leadership style, and if working with a co-worker, any tensions and collusions that have arisen in the course of running the group sessions. In addition you will also need to have a high degree of self-awareness when undertaking groupwork and this can be greatly enhanced within the right supervision environment, helping to identify any prejudicial attitudes, biases and assumptions.

SELF-DIRECTED GROUPS

According to Fleming and Ward (2013: 48–66) self-directed groupwork has its roots in anti-oppressive practice principles and requires a particular type of facilitation of a group. In these groups they suggest there is a blurring of the roles between facilitator and group members. The model is one where the facilitator 'encourages group members to recognise the capabilities', skills, and understanding they possess, with the aim of passing more power and control to the participants as the group progresses. It is further highlighted by Fleming and Ward (2013: 64) that:

> self-directed groupwork has always encapsulated a style of working in which facilitators do not lead the group, but facilitate people in making decisions for themselves and in controlling whatever outcome ensues.

This style of facilitation can be used by social workers most effectively with open-ended groups and can eventually lead to members becoming more confident in their abilities and having less reliance on the original facilitator for the tasks and maintenance of the group. If you are the facilitator of such a group it is likely that your professional involvement as a social worker will necessarily have to be time-limited and that you will need to eventually negotiate your withdrawal from the group. In planning for this time you should make the group aware from the beginning that at some future point you will withdraw from the group, whilst at the same time assuring members that they will be involved in deciding both the timing and manner of this transition process.

CONCLUSION

This chapter has provided a guide to the practical steps and considerations that need to be dealt with prior to setting up a group. It is acknowledged that, for those who already have experience in working with groups, most of what has been covered will be second nature to you. However, for those social workers (or indeed other professionals) who are less experienced in the art of groupwork, running a group for the first time, or at the stage of contemplating doing so, this chapter provides a basic grounding in the planning and preparation required. As has been highlighted in the text, the majority of the planning and preparation will be similar, regardless of what type of group you are running, but there will be some differences depending on the purpose of the group, whether the group has been commissioned by an agency/organisation or is self-directed, and if you are leading or facilitating the group.

Whilst we have highlighted what we regard to be the key issues in planning and preparation for groupwork in this chapter, a number of the issues raised will be examined in more depth in the following chapters, as we move on to setting up the group, exploring the different methods and techniques, and how groupwork practice can be enhanced.

Further reading

Doel, M. (2006) *Using Groupwork*. Abingdon, Oxon: Routledge.
Whilst the above looks at many of the practical considerations necessary when setting up a group, Doel in chapter 3 of his book reflects on the need to strategically 'prepare' for a group by developing alliances and establishing a planning group. He suggests that the leader or facilitator needs to 'prepare' for the unexpected within the group, and rehearse likely difficult scenarios. Doel highlights that any group will benefit from having structured sessions but also stresses the importance of unplanned extra time.

Fleming, J. and Ward, D. (2013) 'Facilitation and groupwork tasks in self-directed groupwork', *Groupwork*, vol. 23, London: Whiting and Birch.
This is a short but interesting abstract which expands on the piece in this chapter about self-directed groupwork, explaining in more detail about the principles behind it and how the concept is being put into practice. It highlights how this form of groupwork can help empower members to achieve their desired outcomes and take control of their own destiny. It also stresses that self-directed groupwork has its roots in anti-oppressive methods of practice.

Thompson, N. (2012) *Anti-Discriminatory Practice* (5th edn). Basingstoke: Palgrave Macmillan in conjunction with BASW.
In this chapter we highlight the need to ensure that as a social worker you work in both an anti-discriminatory and anti-oppressive way in your groupwork practice. If therefore you are interested in exploring further the importance of social justice in society and if you want to learn more about tackling all aspects of discrimination and oppression in your own social work practice, then this book will help to give you a better understanding of what discrimination is in all of its different forms.

5

SETTING UP AND STARTING OUT

Chapter summary

In this chapter you will learn about

- welcome
- opening statement
- introductions
- aims and objectives
- hopes and fears
- ground rules
- ice-breaking exercises
- body of work
- ending the first session
- evaluation and recording

INTRODUCTION

In the previous chapter of this book we focussed on the planning and preparation needed in order to set up a group. As a result we are now ready to move on to consider the mechanics of how you prepare for setting up and starting out on your first groupwork session. Although in the pre-group planning phase you will have done much of the preparation for the group there are still specific issues that you will need to think about prior to the first session. This chapter will highlight what those initial considerations are and take you chronologically through the group setting up and starting out processes.

This chapter will help you with planning your first group session in relation to the structure, technology, types of activities and exercises that you will need to include how to set up the groupwork environment. It will then move on to consider how as leader or facilitator you will manage important aspects of the first session.

SETTING UP

Structure

It will be important in planning for the first session that the leader or facilitator has thought about how the allotted time for the first session will be structured. The usual approach will be to draw up a plan with approximate timings for each element of the proposed programme. The programme is likely to mirror the type of group being run, but whether structured or unstructured in approach, the leader or facilitator will need to ensure that it allows for both flexibility and the space and time for groupwork. The most effective leader or facilitator will be adaptable in their approach and be able to respond to issues that arise or requests from group members, without being diverted away from key elements of the session.

An example of a first session is contained below:

Session 1 (2 ½ hours)

6.20pm – Members Arrive

6.30pm – Welcome & Introductions

6.40pm – Ice-breaking Exercise

7.10pm – Ground Rules

7.30pm – Hopes & Fears Exercise (Pairs/Threes)

7.50pm – Break & Refreshments (20 mins)

8.10pm – Exercise 2

8.40pm – Session Feedback/Review

9.00pm – Close

There is an interesting debate to be had about whether refreshment/comfort breaks are a good thing or not within a group. It is argued on the one hand that they can provide a positive focus that assists the group to get to know each other more quickly and aids cohesion, whereas on the other hand they can disrupt group focus at key times, lead to the formation of sub-groups and distract group process if not managed tightly. The decision about whether to include a break in the programme will need to be made prior to the group commencing and will partially be dictated by the duration of your sessions; with the rule of thumb being if your sessions are over two hours in duration it is likely you will need to include some form of refreshment/comfort break.

Whatever you decide can always be reviewed at a later date with the obvious 'health warning' that if you initially include a break in your programme, this will be difficult to subsequently remove. If refreshments are provided it is important that you convey to members how they can obtain their refreshments, i.e., self-serve or leader/facilitator to serve, etc., and be sure that everyone can obtain a drink, within the designated break. You also need to consider whether you intend to join the group for the break or allow members time on their own.

COMMENT

In our experience it is preferable to allow the group to have a break on their own, as this assists members in getting to know each other better and they are likely to be less inhibited in their conversations.

Information Technology

In the previous chapter we made mention of information technology (IT) and the roles it can play in the groupwork process. However we wanted to further acknowledge some of the opportunities and disadvantages that IT can potentially provide within groups.

According to Simon and Stauber (2011: 7–21), 'a large percentage of today's groupworkers were educated before the development of theses formats …' and that 'while email communication has become widely accepted, many skilled practitioners and educators feel overwhelmed by the technical skills required to conduct online groups'.

They suggest that whilst once upon a time it was only possible to carry out groupwork on a face-to-face basis, due to the advances in IT there are now opportunities resulting from 'new platforms for communication' which include 'internet chat groups, telephone groups, online support groups and other virtual groups' that can be utilised. These technologies allow for virtual groupwork to take place with the leader posting material which is then discussed online by members, and may or may not involve the group meeting for a face-to-face session. It is also possible for group members to be supported by using IT that provides the opportunity for the setting up of online forums, uploading communications, exercises, video materials and other information.

Although you will not all be running a virtual group you can still employ some of the IT highlighted above, but you need to be sure that any technology used enhances rather than detracts from the groupwork experience being offered. The use of IT with the likes of mobile phones, tablets, laptops can clearly both improve communication and increase the opportunities for the leader and members to creatively explore and share information within and outside the group setting.

The disadvantages with IT include the fact that if it is not used appropriately it can actually disrupt the interaction and flow of the group and so, as suggested previously, should be used sparingly. Another disadvantage is the additional time you may need to spend in order to familiarise yourself with the technology you intend to use, as there is nothing worse than a group sitting for ten minutes while you struggle to get a film clip to play, etc. The Internet also provides easy access for any member to look up a particular exercise you may have mentioned that you intend to use at a future session and this could potentially spoil the experience you are seeking to create for members coming to it afresh. Finally you need to be aware, as leader, that it is inevitable that some group members will seek to exchange mobile phone numbers and have contact with each other in between sessions, and this can on occasions have a detrimental impact on the dynamics within the group.

Activities

Whatever programme you draw up for the first or subsequent sessions it is likely to contain activities, but as highlighted above it is important to maintain a balance between structured activity and unstructured or unscripted space for spontaneous development of the group. If you are the person that has convened the group it is inevitable (even with self-directed groups) that at the initial session members will look to you to provide leadership about the programme and the way forward. It is tempting sometimes, in order to allay your own anxieties, to try and cram too many activities or exercises into the first session to prevent the group process falling flat. However as you grow in confidence in managing these groups you will learn how best to structure sessions and can always prepare material that you hold in reserve should IT equipment fail to operate on the night, or an activity end sooner than anticipated.

The content of the groupwork sessions will be determined by the type of group being run and whether you are delivering an 'off-the-shelf' programme following a predetermined format or a 'bespoke' one that you will need to design from scratch. If it is the latter, or you are simply looking for ways of enhancing the existing set-up, there is an almost endless range of different activities, games and exercises that you could use in the initial, and indeed subsequent sessions. These have been categorised in a host of different ways over the years but according to Whitaker (1992: 126–7) includes:

- **Participative** – An activity, game or exercise 'done for its own sake, for an intrinsic appeal to those that participate in it' for the purpose of 'pleasure and enjoyment...'
- **Interactive** – An activity, game or exercise that 'is expected to generate interactions between participants which can be utilised as a basis for intervention ... directed towards benefiting individuals'.
- **Role Play** – An activity, game or exercise that 'constitutes a rehearsal in a protected environment for something the individual wishes to do or will have to do later in the outside world'.

- **Related** – An activity, game or exercise that 'is intended to be an easy or palatable step towards understanding ... something else'.
- **Engineered** – An activity, game or exercise that 'is an alternative route ... to something which could otherwise occur in open discussion'.
- **Accelerated** – An activity, game or exercise which 'is meant to make something which one expects or hopes to happen anyway, happen faster'.
- **Empathy** – An activity, game or exercise which is designed 'to help persons to empathise with others with whom they interact and whose view they do not ordinarily take into account'.

Perhaps a simpler list of activity types is highlighted by Douglas (1991b: 49–50) when he suggests that for most groups a combination of the following activities is likely to be used: *play* (games); *drama and role-play*; *talk* (discussion/speakers/conversations etc.); *movement* (dance/mime/physical encounter); *work* (co-operative endeavour/working together to achieve the task)…

It should not be forgotten that the types of activities or exercises used with a group may well be partially or even fully dictated by those service users involved in the planning process or by group members as the sessions develop. A list of games and activity resources are included at the end of this chapter in the further reading.

Environment

Although it may sound obvious it is imperative that the person co-ordinating the group arrives at the venue for the first session in good time, to ensure that everything is in place prior to members' arrival. In the authors' experience there have been occasions where those responsible for the venue have unfortunately forgotten you are coming and you find the building not open or the heating not turned on. As in life, first impressions are important and you will want group members attending the first session to feel welcome (see below); and on a cold winter's night an open, well-lit and warm environment is a good start to any group.

Once at the venue you will need to ensure the chairs are put out into the desired arrangement, so that all groupworkers and members have a chair. It is also important to ensure that each chair within the circle formation is of a reasonable quality, as there is nothing worse than one member of the group having to sit on a broken or damaged chair for the duration of the group.

COMMENT

In some groups run by the authors it has been their custom to always put out enough chairs for the whole group, regardless of whether any members are absent, as this reminds those attending that absentees are still considered as part of the group even if not present.

LEADERSHIP AND FACILITATION STYLES

A final consideration before you move on to 'starting out' with the group is the way in which you intend to lead or facilitate the group. The co-ordination and leadership role within a group can sometimes be a difficult task and when problems or issues arise it is likely that you will revert to your default or typical leadership style.

Let us then take a moment to think about the various aspects of leadership and facilitation, so that you can reflect on the various styles and traits and will be able recognise them at any given point in the groupwork process. What is certain is that in order to be an effective leader or facilitator you are likely to have to alternate between different leadership styles during each session and indeed the life of the group itself.

According to Lawler and Bilson (2010: 35–43) the author Gill states that 'no theory or model of leadership so far has provided a satisfactory explanation of leadership; indeed there is no consensus on the meaning of leadership in the first place'. Having said this there have nevertheless been a variety of different theories and models over the years that have sought to shed light on this area. A number of these are summarised on the Mind Tools website (2014, http://www.mindtools.com/pages/article/leadership-theories.htm) (although we have added some of our own) and these include:

Theories
McGregor's Theory X and Y

This theory suggests that Theory X leaders assume that individuals dislike hard work, avoid responsibility and need to be controlled or supervised in order for the work to be completed. As one may imagine they tend to be leaders who seek to control members, do not delegate and maintain control over all aspects of the process. However, Theory Y leaders assume that individuals are self-motivated, creative and enjoy taking responsibility. As a result Theory Y leaders are more participative with members and allow them to take greater responsibility for decisions.

Contingency model

This theory suggests that leadership is linked to situational variables and that the leader will need to adopt a task-orientated style in certain situations and a relationship style in others.

Trait theory

This is a model that suggests that leaders are born rather than made, or at least share some key characteristics or behaviour traits. Although there has been research that discredits its basis, it remains popular in some quarters.

Leadership styles

Lewin – three major leadership styles

Although dating back to the 1930s psychologist Kurt Lewin's work is still a simple way of identifying types of leadership style which comprise of:

- **Autocratic** – leaders make decisions without consulting members and maintain almost total power and control over the group. Members can become disaffected as they feel powerless and that things are being done to them.
- **Democratic** – leaders make ultimate decisions but include members in the decision-making process, sharing power and control with the group. Members are likely to be more engaged in the group process and feel they have a stake in achieving the process. This approach can be less effective in making quick decisions. (The Democratic leadership style is the favoured approach for most social workers running groups.)
- **Laissez-faire** – leaders let members work out for themselves how they want to go about achieving tasks and provide support and resources if needed, but otherwise do not get involved. Members feel they have autonomy over tasks but problems can occur if they do not have the resources or skills to complete the task, and may feel frustration at the perceived lack of guidance and support they receive.

Bureaucratic leadership

These are leaders who do things by the book, following the rules to the letter and do not deviate from the agreed programme or task. Although highly useful in high-risk situations, they tend to stifle group creativity and do not allow for group contribution.

Transformational leadership

In recent years transformational leadership has become very popular and relies on the leader having a clear vision for his group or team and then using a range of behaviours to motivate, inspire and stimulate members to be innovative and creative. These leaders will develop the trust of members by putting their needs before his/her own and supporting/empowering them to make decisions towards achieving their goal.

Transactional leadership

This type of leadership relies on members effectively agreeing to do whatever the leader tells them in return for identified rewards/benefits. Members are judged on their performance of the task and overall contribution, with the notion that if they fail to meet the appropriate standard then they will be sanctioned. Consequently members who perform well are rewarded and reap the benefits for their hard work. The limitations of this approach tend to be that it restricts individual and creative applications to the task in hand.

FACILITATION

In Chapter 4 we discussed the differences and similarities between a leader and a facilitator, highlighting some of the shared functions and obvious differences between the roles. In researching this book the authors note that whilst there is a significant amount that has been written with regard to group leadership styles, there is much less in relation to approaches to facilitation. This may be because it is assumed that as a facilitator you will be using many of the same skills utilised in leadership and hence adopt some of the same styles.

In her book *The Personal Development Group* Rose (2008: 2) highlights that:

> The role of the facilitator is complex and the manner in which it is performed is highly influential in the development of the group.

Although leadership encompasses characteristics like being directive to a greater or lesser degree, asserting control and setting agendas, the facilitator's role is more about enabling members to achieve their own goals. As a consequence the facilitator's approach to groupwork will mean that they are likely to speak significantly less than a leader, as they do not seek to impose their own agenda or opinions on members to the same degree. The facilitator then will help to lead discussion in the group, but also encourages reflection, and supports members to take the lead; as highlighted in the previous chapter, with self-directed groups the facilitator would be looking to a time when they can negotiate their own exit and leave the group to run itself.

COMMENT

In many ways facilitating a group can be more difficult than leading it, as it requires the facilitator to be comfortable in relinquishing much of their control over the group, its agenda and shared goals and to be led more by the members' wishes and what develops from the process.

STARTING OUT

According to Benson (2001: 48–9):

> The first session and indeed the early phase of any group is a crucial time for individual members and is critical in determining how subsequent patterns of interaction and communication unfold within the group.

He goes on to suggest that that 'the first session is the moment of social and psychological birth for the group' and consequently the importance in getting this process right is clearly self-evident.

During the following paragraphs of this chapter we will take you through the various aspects of 'starting out' the group and explain what is required of you as a leader or facilitator during the first groupwork session. Although the book has previously considered a range of different group types for the purposes of clarity, within the remaining chapters all mention of 'group' and 'group process' should be taken as referring to a 'closed, fixed-term group' run with a leader.

The welcome

However confident we are as individuals, joining any new group is likely to arouse a range of anxieties and fears in us, which are hard to ignore. It is important therefore that as leaders and facilitators we recognise that such feelings are likely to be shared to a greater or lesser degree by all members attending the first group session. These feelings will no doubt have been fuelled by members' own previous experiences of groups, whether good or bad, and any preconceived ideas or fantasies they may have about what is likely to emerge in the sessions to follow. It may also be coloured by whether members' attendance at the group is through choice, professional nomination, or they have been required to attend as a result of a court order or mandatory element of their training course.

As a consequence the authors view the welcome to the first session as both a continuation of the pre-group contracting process and an important element in its own right. The welcome to the group is essentially split into three different parts, which are: the initial welcome, the environment, and the group welcome.

When members first arrive at the group and walk through the door, it is important that the leader or facilitator is there to greet them with a smile and a few words of welcome. It helps make members feel that their presence at the group is valued and assists them to make a 'connection' or 're-connection' with the leader or facilitator, who they would hopefully have met in the pre-group contracting process. The welcome also sets the tone for the group as a whole and will encourage members to feel that they want to return to future sessions.

The next issue is the significance of a welcoming environment which was briefly touched upon in Chapter 4 when we considered pre-group 'Planning and Preparation' tasks. Therefore it is important that the venue you have chosen for the group is an appropriately decorated, well-lit, warm and inviting environment, where members can feel at ease in each other's presence. The environment should reflect the purpose of the group and so choices can be made about the level of lighting, whether low-level background music is initially played, and the arrangement of chairs.

Finally once members are gathered and the session begins, as the leader of the group the onus will be on you to formally welcome attendees to the group. What you say is a matter of personal preference but it is important to make members feel both welcome and at ease, prior to any 'opening statement'. We suggest the formal welcome is brief but sincere and to give you an idea we have included a suggested short welcome statement.

'Good evening to you all. My name, as most of you will remember, is Karl. It's such an unpleasant evening out there with the weather, so it is really nice to see you all here tonight, and can I start by welcoming you to the first session of the group. In a moment we will begin with some group introductions, but first I want to talk a little bit about the group itself and what we will be doing in sessions to come.'

COMMENT

There are occasions when the décor or other aspects of the venue you have chosen or been allocated are not up to the standards you would want for the group. When this is the case you will have little choice other than to simply acknowledge this fact but should be cautious about becoming too apologetic, as essentially these are issues beyond your control and may be interpreted by the group in a variety of unhelpful ways.

OPENING STATEMENT

The opening statement is referred to by Doel (2006: 64) as the leader or facilitator placing their 'cards on the table' and suggests it is their opportunity to help members understand why 'the group is worthwhile'. He goes on to propose that whilst it is actually a 're-statement of the individual offer of groupwork' it is nevertheless 'symbolically important to make it to everyone at the same time' in order to ensure that everybody hears the same message.

As highlighted above, the opening statement is a chance for you to share with members why the group has been set up and what it seeks to achieve, or in other words the purpose of the group. It is also an opportunity to reiterate to members the practical arrangements for the group including dates, times, session structure and planned breaks. The opening statement is a useful vehicle to tell the group something about yourself (personal statement) and the reason you are involved in leading/facilitating the group. Although you should try to incorporate information the group are likely to require, you should expect and indeed invite questions from members after finishing the opening statement. However, you need to ensure that this is achieved in a concise manner and the process does not derail the task in hand.

In addition to the issues outlined above, the leader or facilitator will need to deal with health and safety issues in terms of fire safety (including exits and any scheduled fire drills, etc.), toilet locations and venue related issues.

Finally there will, as highlighted above, be a variety of different feelings in the room about the group process (as well as external factors) and as leader or facilitator you should try to acknowledge in the opening statement that it is perfectly normal for members to feel this way. It is hoped that by acknowledging this fact members will feel less anxious and more able to focus on the session to follow.

INTRODUCTIONS

The process of introducing a group of individuals who do not know each other should, you would think, be a fairly straightforward process. However there are, we suggest, some ways of introduction that are better than others and getting it right can prove a significant benefit in terms of helping to develop group cohesion at this early stage.

Firstly it should not be forgotten that sitting in a circle with a group of strangers may conjure up the same sort of apprehensive feelings that some members felt on their first day of attending a new school. They are anxious and out of their comfort zone and the thought of speaking in front of the whole group may well fill some with fear, although this of course may not be universally the case. Therefore when you as leader or facilitator step forward in all innocence and ask members to introduce themselves to the rest of the group, maybe saying something about their background and perhaps what they hope to get out of attending the group, for some this may prove both threatening and difficult. Figure 5.1 below illustrates this process, which the authors have heard referred to as the 'creeping death' introduction, as you slowly get more and more anxious as you wait for your turn to speak.

It is useful then to take a moment to consider what it is that you want to achieve from the introductions process within the group. Firstly there is the obvious in that you want everyone to know each other's names and ideally you want everybody to be able to remember the names of all those other members. Secondly, it is useful for each member to share a small piece of personal information with the group as this signifies that they are prepared to give up something of themselves to the collective group. Although early in the group process it can also be interesting for both the

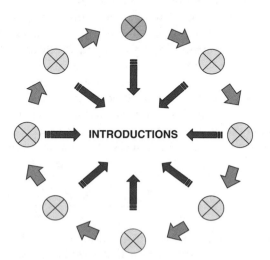

Figure 5.1

leader/facilitator and the group itself to hear what members are wanting or hoping to get out of the group experience.

There are then a range of ways that you can achieve the above without making it too daunting for new members and below are some suggestions of activities and exercises that may help you in this respect.

Introduce your partner – A very simple way of taking the pressure off individuals is to get them into pairs or groups of three (depending on the numbers) and to give them the task of talking to each other for 2–3 minutes about themselves and then swapping over. They are tasked to discover their partner's name, where they were born and their favourite colour; and what the members are asked can clearly be adapted to meet your preferences.

My Name Is – Another way of obtaining information is to get the group to sit or stand in a circle with the leader or facilitator standing in the middle. The leader or facilitator then introduces the game by saying that they will throw the ball (a foam one is good, but any ball can be used) to a random member of the group who will shout out their name saying 'My name is … Noah, Maisie, Sophia, Josh,' etc. Once the member has had their turn the ball is thrown back to the leader or facilitator who throws it randomly to someone else in the group, and so on until all members have introduced themselves. The game can be extended by the leader or facilitator stepping out of the centre and joining members in the circle. The game continues with the person holding the ball shouting out 'Your name is ... Shanice' and then throwing the ball to that member. They then throw the ball to another member until everyone in the group has been named in turn. There may be occasions when a number of members' names have been forgotten so they will be asked by the leader or facilitator to remind the group of their name.

Written Names – There are occasions when an individual member or indeed members, will find that their own anxiety gets in the way of them being able to hear and retain information during the first session. In order to pre-empt this you may decide to provide members with some form of written aide during the first and possibly subsequent sessions. This can be achieved in a number of ways including getting members to write their names on large sticky labels, which you ask them to wear during the first couple of sessions. Another way in which individuals can be helped is by the leader or facilitator asking each member their name and then writing it down on flip-chart paper which can be displayed in a prominent position. A variation on this is suggested by Doel and Sawdon (1999: 146/7) by means of writing down members' names on the flip-chart in a circle, in the order that they currently sit in the group. The information can then be added to at a later time as members' expectations of the group are revealed.

COMMENT

It is important when planning your introduction process that you ensure that it meets the needs of all participants within that specific group. There will be occasions when you have a group member or members with a disability and will need to ensure that the design of introduction activities/exercises does not exclude them from participating.

AIMS AND OBJECTIVES

Although the overall purpose of the group (e.g., improving parenting) will have been restated by the leader during the opening statement, the aims and objectives are about what individuals, and the group, are seeking to achieve and the actions required to get there. Whilst it can be argued that the aims and objectives will usually flow from the purpose, it does need to be recognised that they can be both overt and covert in nature and may change over the life of the group.

The first question then will be who decides the aims and objectives for the group and is this solely the leader, the leader and members jointly, or just the members. According to Brown (1994: 63):

> The degree of negotiability will vary according to the particular model…

He suggests that there are three types of groupwork model to describe the negotiation process in relation to decision making in a group and these are:

- Low Negotiability – where worker power is high and member power low
- Medium Negotiability – where there is more equality between worker and member power
- High Negotiability – where member power is high and worker power low

The way in which you go about identifying the aims and objectives for the group will to some degree flow from the purpose of the group and how much you want members involved in shaping its content and direction. In a self-directed groupwork for instance you would expect there to be 'high negotiability' around the group aims and objectives, whereas in a group for sex offenders – who are directed to attend by court order – there may be 'low negotiability' in this area.

As leader it will be your decision as to how you go about identifying the aims and objectives for the group. However, if you want members to be involved in this process a good way to start is to get members divided into pairs or threes, depending on the size of the group, and then ask them what they want to achieve from the following sessions. The members can then feedback in their pairs or threes and you can write up their various individual and group aims and objectives. However, it is worth compiling some of your own, just in case the group struggles at this early stage in the group process and in order to list those things that are non-negotiable. Once the aims and objectives are set you should consider whether you will keep them displayed, give a copy to each member or at the very least refer back to them prior to the conclusion of the group, and in order to prepare for the final evaluation process.

HOPES AND FEARS

As highlighted above when bringing together a number of individuals for the purposes of a group it is natural that they will arrive with a whole range of different views and feelings concerning the first session, including some that will be influenced or impacted upon by previous experiences and current issues in their lives. Consequently it is useful when 'starting out' to have an understanding of what members expect to obtain from the group and what they are worried about, which are commonly termed 'hopes and fears'. It is likely that members' anxieties will be commonly shared across the group and some of these are not difficult to anticipate, such as a fear of speaking in front of the group. In fact Doel and Sawdon (1999: 95–7) talk about the importance of the person co-ordinating the group 'tuning in' to the 'emotions and feelings' of both individuals and the group as a whole.

There are once again a number of ways to elicit the 'hopes and fears' of group members, including going around the group and asking for individuals contributions and writing them on a flip-chart. An alternative method would be to get members to discuss their 'hopes and fears' in pairs and then obtain feedback on an individual or collective basis; or to get each member to write down their hopes and fears anonymously on a piece of paper, which is deposited in a container for the leader/facilitator to pick out and read. Whatever method used it will be important that the leader, during the process, provides some commentary to ensure that all contributions are acknowledged as valued and important to the group.

Whilst all individuals will come to the group with anxieties in one form or another, the better these are managed within the first group session the more likely it is that members will engage productively in the subsequent sessions.

Activity 5.1

In most groupwork literature it is recognised that the majority of people will join a group with some degree of anxiety about what is to follow. This may emanate from their previous experiences in groups or simply from a fear of making themselves vulnerable within discussions taking place in the group.

What do you consider to be some of the anxieties a person may bring to the group and how might these manifest themselves within the sessions?

COMMENT

A person's anxieties may affect them in a range of different ways and they may express these by being silent, or contributing very little during discussions. Although each individual is different this may have resulted from them never being able to find their voice, always being shouted down in their family of origin or being overlooked at school. It is equally as likely that the person's anxieties may result in them display-ing other behaviours including talking excessively, being disruptive or acting out in some way.

GROUND RULES

When bringing members together in order to form a group they will come with their own experiences of right and wrong, acceptable and unacceptable behaviour, which may or may not be consistent with others in the group. Each individual will also arrive having already made a decision either consciously or unconsciously about whether they wish be part of the group or not, including their level of ongoing com-mitment and communication within the process. It is important then from the start to establish a set of shared and consistent ground rules with members so that the group is able to function effectively and create a safe space for the groupwork to take place.

According to Doel (2006: 69):

> The ground rules are rather like the constitution for the group – a statement of mutual expectations, an agreement about what is acceptable and not acceptable, and possibly what sanctions may be invoked if they are breached.

The ground rules are something that require negotiation with members at the first session and are the final part of the group contracting process with those individuals. Once the ground rules have been established they may need to be revisited several times during the life of the group to renegotiate or clarify particular points. Whilst it is possible for the leader to impose pre-written ground rules upon the group this is generally not seen as good practice for in order for members to own the rules they must have responsibility for, and have been involved in, negotiating them. During the negotiation process it is also important to agree what sanctions will be put in place if members of the group breach any of the ground rules.

It is not possible to talk about the negotiation of ground rules without considering the issue of power and authority in the process. The leader is often the one person in the group who will have previous experience of devising ground rules and this is likely to afford them some real or perceived power or authority over members when it comes to negotiation. Furthermore members may look to the leader to offer suggestions or guidance in setting the ground rules, if they are struggling with ideas. Members will naturally retain the power to either contribute, or not, to the ground rule-setting process, and even endeavour to push through particular rules that they consider to be to their own advantage.

When describing the process Lindsay and Orton (2011: 105) state:

> Taking time in the first session for exploring, negotiating and deciding ground rules, and perhaps thinking about how decisions are to be made in the group, is a good way of exploring some issues of power. Every group will have "rules" whether spoken or not, and it can be empowering to raise this issue and to allow discussion and negotiation.

Whilst it is possible for some groups to manage with more general rules, establishing specific ground rules and boundaries at this early stage can save valuable time later in the group process. It is important to write these rules up and ensure that members have access to them at each session via either flip-chart paper, or distributing them to members in printed form or via email.

Case study

Chris (leader) had not anticipated that so many ground rules would be suggested by the group in the first session and was pleased to see that all the members were happy to agree to them. However, ten minutes into the session someone's mobile phone rang and the group member decided to answer it (in contravention of the agreed ground rules), clearly making arrangements for the weekend.

How would you deal with this situation if it arose in a group you were running?

COMMENT

Chris decided to make it clear through gestures to the member in question that the call needed to end and when he came off the phone, asked what had prompted him to answer the call. He also went on to ask the group how they had felt about the member's actions in terms of answering his mobile during the session.

Activity 5.2

You are the leader of a new group being run and during the first session you ask members for their suggestions for ground rules. From your previous experience of groups what would you expect to see in the list of negotiated ground rules?

COMMENT

Although no two groups are the same, in the authors' experience the ground rules are likely to include expectations around some of the following areas:

- Confidentiality
- Time Keeping
- Respect
- Honesty
- Silence

- Eating/drinking
- Mobile Phones
- Absences
- Endings

Although the above list is far from comprehensive it covers some of the main ground rules that you would expect to see in most groups. However, confidentiality is perhaps one of the key ground rules as it helps to establish clear boundaries for members both within and outside the group. It also provides a safe space where individuals can explore and share their concerns and anxieties without the fear that it will be shared with others inappropriately. Another ground rule that needs careful consideration and negotiation is whether members are able to opt out of particular exercises or activities, and if so the basis for this.

ICE-BREAKING EXERCISES

Having safely negotiated the group welcome, opening statement, introductions, hopes and fears exercise, and ground rules, it is time to move on to your first ice-breaking exercise. It is possible that at this stage in the first session members are still quite anxious or some even withdrawn and therefore you need to try to change the dynamic in the group. Ice-breaking exercises are designed to ease the tension in the room and promote interaction between members, ensuring that individuals get to know one another better. The exercises also promote trust and better communication between members, develop teamwork and a sense of group cohesion. However, they also provide the opportunity for some physical and fun-based activities.

It is further highlighted by Benson (2010: 71) that 'there is a wide range of games and exercises designed to accelerate the process of inclusion...'

A good source is *The New Youth Games Handbook* (Dearling and Armstrong, 1994: 13–55) which although a little dated includes a whole section on group games and ice-breaking exercises which can be adapted. They even suggest that you should 'always try to have something up your sleeve' in terms of games or exercises in case other things proceed too quickly or fall flat. In addition the book contains a planning checklist which reminds groupworkers about the importance of planning the games, exercises and activities within sessions, taking into account the needs of members and their ability to interact. Whilst there is not sufficient time within this chapter to describe many of the ice-breaking exercises, here are a couple of examples either from the book or activities we have used:

- The Ball Game

  A version of this game/exercise is described above in Introductions.

- The Name Game

  An exercise where members are asked to tell the story of their name, in terms of how and what they were named, whether they like their name, and whether they were named after someone else, etc.

- Group Sort

  A game aimed at getting members to interact to complete a task. In this game members are asked by the leader to sort themselves into a single line based alphabetically on their first name or some other characteristic.

Finally it needs to be stressed that it is crucial when selecting a particular game or exercise for the first session that it needs to be something that will assist group members to make a meaningful contact with each other.

Case study

Beth decided that she would use the 'ball game' as both an ice-breaker and following the intro-ductions, in order to help the group members learn and remember each other's names. She started with each member throwing the ball to someone else, saying their own name as they threw it. The game progressed with Beth encouraging members to say both their own name and the name of the person they were throwing it to. However, she was aware that there was one member of the group who persistently got the names of everybody else wrong.
How would you deal with this situation?

COMMENT

Thankfully the member who found it difficult to remember other people's names had a good sense of humour, as did the other members of the group. The net result was that group members opted to wear name badges for the first few weeks until everyone had established better relationships with each other and got to know one another's names.

BODY OF WORK

Whilst it can be tempting for any leader to move straight into group process (body of work) it is nevertheless vital that the preliminary steps described above are under-taken in order to provide a solid foundation for the groupwork to follow.

This is the part of the first session when the group, through discussion, exercises or activities, makes a start on addressing the issues and reasons for them being there. It is common for the leader to arrive at this point in the first session having more or less time in terms of the programme than they had originally envisaged. As a result you will need to be flexible in your approach and ensure that you involve members (where appropriate) in deciding how they wish to use the remaining time. The importance of being prepared for these occasions by having additional discussion topics, exercises or activities in reserve is vital.

An example of a discussion topic that could be used with any group, called '*situations*', is described by Dearling and Armstrong (1994: 97) as being a useful technique to encourage members to look at particular difficult social situations. The exercise requires a group of cards to be prepared in advance by the leader with a range of dilemmas written on them. Each member then selects a card and in turn reads it out to the group, stating how they would respond to the situation; the remaining group members are then invited by the leader to give their views on the matter. What is written on the cards will depend on the type of group being run but could include:

'You ask for cashback at the local supermarket when buying your food shopping and discover on the way out of the store that the cashier has given you £20 too much in change. Do you go back into the store and return the money, or simply keep it?'

What you should be seeing at this stage in the group is that members start to interact with each other towards those individual and group goals. It is suggested by Vernelle (1994: 28) that 'the interactions that develop between the individuals and the group, produce the process. Every group has a particular way of developing and working'.

In our experience the body of the work can develop in a number of ways and as leader you need to be aware of how the process within the group is being taken forward. Firstly, you may see a group where members are compliant with the exercise or activity, but only interact in a superficial way within this initial session. This is not anything to worry about necessarily at this early stage unless it continues into the later sessions. Secondly, you may see a group where members fully engage and interact with the process and appear to make progress in addressing the set goals. Lastly is the group where you have a mixture of members, some who superficially engage, some who appear to engage well and one or more who undermine the process with their lack of engagement or disruptive behaviour. Whichever scenario unfolds the advice is the same, namely to reflect upon what has happened in the group, consider your role in the process and most importantly don't be disheartened if the group is not progressing in the way you had envisaged. Furthermore Benson (2010: 43) reminds us, that workers should 'remember, while it is nice to get everything right in the first session it is not always possible and you will have plenty of opportunities in subsequent sessions to redeem and salvage lost ground'.

ENDING THE FIRST SESSION

The importance of endings is something that we will explore further in subsequent chapters but firstly we need to consider how best to end the first session.

The expectation is that the subject of 'endings' will have been something covered to some extent within the ground rules exercise and as part of the first session group contracting process.

It is obvious then that for an ending to be useful it needs in some way to meet the expectations of group members you are working with. These individuals will have had their own good, bad and indifferent experiences of endings and therefore they will all have expectations of what constitutes a positive or useful ending. This said, a universally good tip for ending the first session is to ensure that it ends on time, for in this way it will help to reinforce to the group that you are a person of your word, as well as someone who can be trusted and that the group itself has clear boundaries and structure. The next tip is to allow an amount of time prior to the end of the session in order to summarise what has been achieved, manage expectations for the following week and confirm the time and venue details.

There are occasions when, as leader, you will be faced with the dilemma of what to do when an individual is talking about a particularly difficult or painful issue at the end of the session. The choices are to let them continue and extend the session or simply to curtail what they are saying with the aim of finishing the group on time. This has to be your call as leader and will of course depend on the importance or relevance of what they are saying. If this occurs in the first group session extending the ending of the group may be accepted by members as a one-off, but if it occurs more than once it may be a sign that the group has a more serious problem with endings, and this will need to be addressed.

It may be useful to keep an amount of time at the end in order to summarise what has been achieved in the first session and manage expectations for the following week, providing a bridge to the second session. This can be the point where you seek feedback on the session from those present and also clarify that all members are able to attend the next group meeting. Groups can sometimes decide to get members' views and opinions on the session or the way in which they are feeling about the group by using the concept of 'checking in' and 'checking out'. This is simply a device for helping members get in touch with the group process at the start and make any comments that they want to about group process or content before they finish the session.

As a final piece of advice it is useful to try and finish each groupwork session on a positive note and, if appropriate, thank members for their contribution and state that you look forward to seeing everyone at the next session.

Case study

James had set up a group for people who had criminal convictions and had anticipated that the group would run for three hours every Monday night for a duration of six weeks. The group started at 5.00pm and ran through until 8.00pm, so James planned at around 7.45pm to start bringing the session to a close in order to let members adjust to the 'real world'. However, at 8.10pm he was still there trying to end the session, as one member of the group felt she needed to tell everyone why she had committed her offences.

What might you have done differently in these circumstances?

COMMENT

This behaviour is not untypical of those people who feel that their needs haven't been met in the group, who believe that they are special in some way, or who feel the need to push (or indeed enjoy pushing) boundaries. These issues need to be dealt with in a sensitive but firm way.

EVALUATION AND RECORDING

When carrying out an evaluation of the first session there are a number of ways of approaching the task, all of which have their advantages and disadvantages. One method is to incorporate seeking feedback from group members towards the end of the session, as part of the programme, but this needs to be carefully considered in terms of any potential disruption to the process. Another way of undertaking the evaluation will be for the leader and any co-facilitator/s to sit down after the group and reflect on how the session went.

The notion of recording the first and subsequent group sessions may not fill you with the same enthusiasm as actually running the group, but it is something that is worth approaching in a systematic way. A record of each group session can be useful in assisting you in feeding back to commissioners and members, in evaluating progress and helping to develop future practice.

It is suggested that you develop a simple format for recording the session which may incorporate any planning and preparation, the outline plan for the session, an overview of what went well and less well, group dynamics (including any initial pairings, alliances and defined roles), process, conflict, responses to the leader and general observations at this early stage. Although we will be discussing many of these concepts in more depth in subsequent chapters, it is important that, as leader, you observe what is happening in the group and take time to record your observations.

Activity 5.3

Whilst the thinking about evaluation and recording will have started at the planning stage for the group, it is only after the first session that the processes and dynamics really begin to show themselves. As highlighted above there are a number of different aspects that you will need to concentrate on in order to gain a full picture of what is going on in the group when carrying out your evaluation and recording. However, one area that is often neglected is the impact the group has upon you as a leader and the influence you may have on the group.

Consider ways in which you influence the group and the impact the group has upon you as its leader.

CONCLUSION

There is clearly a range of issues that must be considered in relation to running the first session. The chapter starts by reminding you about ensuring that you have drawn up a structure for the first session in terms of a detailed plan with timings. It also discusses the use of IT within groups and the possibility of convening virtual groups. The text outlines the importance of making sure that the environment is ready for the group to arrive and then considers the various leadership/facilitation styles and theories you may employ. We then move on to the setting-up phase with the welcome given to group members by the leader at a number of different levels, before discussing what should be said in the opening statement. A variety of ways are highlighted for addressing the important process of member introductions within the group, followed by the aims and objectives – both individual and of the group as a whole – and the hopes and fears. The chapter then describes the process of developing ground rules within the group and how you use ice-breaking exercises to relieve anxiety and tension. Once the introductory tasks are complete the group process moves on to the 'body of the work' and starts to consider the reasons why members have attended the group. Finally we provide you with suggestions about how to end the first session and complete the necessary evaluation and recording.

Further reading

Bergart, A., Simon, S. and Doel, M. (2012) *Group Work: Honouring Our Roots, Nurturing Our Growth*. London: Whiting and Birch.
The book is an edited collection of papers from the 2009 Annual International Symposium of the Association for the Advancement of Social Work with Groups. Chapter 4 of the book looks at the use of programmes and how activities are a method of helping individuals to be able to socialise with other people. In chapter 11, entitled 'Groupwork and Technology: Embracing our Future' the authors consider the arguments in relation to whether workers should embrace what technology has to offer in creating online groups and communities.

Carter, J. (2011) *Over 600 Ice-breakers & Games*. London: Hope Books Ltd.
This book is one of the more recent publications that provide off the shelf ice-breaking activities and team building games, which can be utilised and/or adapted by any group leader or facilitator. It is organised into fourteen different themes and covers issues like getting to know you, feelings and emotions, looking back at the past, and hopes and fears.

Dearling, A. and Armstrong, H. (1994) *The New Youth Games Handbook*. Lyme Regis: Russell House Publishing Ltd.
This is an old but useful book that has a host of ice-breaking exercises, puzzles and games that again can be used and adapted in working with groups by leaders and facilitators.

Although it has youth in the title and does have some games which are aimed at younger children, most of the exercises and games can be used with any age group.

Houston, G. (1993) *The Red Book of Groups*. Aylsham: M.F. Barnwell & Sons.
Once again this is a very old and indeed short text that takes the reader through all aspects of groupwork in a simplistic way, including the process of starting the group and developing their leadership skills. It is not an academic tome but instead concentrates on providing the would-be leader with practical advice and guidance about groups, along with a smattering of games and exercises.

6

FACILITATING – METHODS AND TECHNIQUES

Chapter summary

In this chapter you will learn about

- activities and interventions
- group stages
- cultural aspects of groups
- group dynamics
- roles and behaviours
- power/confrontation and challenge
- scapegoating/collusion/silence/conflict
- self-awareness/difference
- supervision
- themes

INTRODUCTION

Having completed the group planning and preparation, and with first session behind you, the time has come to move on and consider what we term as the working life or 'core phase' of the group, exploring some of the behaviours and roles you may experience. Although in the previous two chapters it was possible to cover the various topics in a linear or chronological manner, in this chapter we need to take a different approach in order to explain what takes place as the group moves past the first session. In the text we will introduce you to various groupwork notions and concepts, discussing how these may manifest themselves and the resulting consequences, and provide you with ideas about how you might manage such situations when they arise within the group.

In essence, from the second session on you will be seeking to take individual members and the group forward in terms of further exploration of the main theme or purpose. This will require you as leader to continue planning the sessions to follow, even if your group is running on a less structured or self-directed model. The material you use for this is likely to continue to be provided via a combination of discussion topics, activities, exercises, role plays, speakers, film and video clips, etc.

The groupwork task then, is made up of two distinct parts, namely the content and the process, and whilst you cannot afford to neglect content planning, as leader you will also need to be able to recognise what is happening in terms of group process, which is what we will be concentrating on for much of this chapter. Whilst the term content is self-explanatory in that it refers to the range of activities, exercises and materials that you use as part of every groupwork session, group process is something that, according to Lindsay and Orton (2011: 69), '... happens below the surface. It can rarely be seen or heard but can nevertheless, be experienced and felt'. It is further explained by Doel (2006: 59) who suggests that 'group processes are patterns of behaviour which form in a group over a period of time and which are usually larger than the behaviour patterns of individual members'.

In the following paragraphs we will begin to further explore the notions of content and process within the groupwork setting.

ACTIVITIES AND INTERVENTIONS

In Chapter 4 we described certain approaches that could be taken to help get the group started and encourage members to begin to get to know each other. Therefore in continuing this theme this chapter will briefly review ways of using activities and interventions to explore aspects of individual and group behaviour to help you move the group through those difficult issues/phases, confront and challenge perceptions and assumptions, and in doing so enable the aims and objectives of the group to be met.

Before considering which activities to use, it is necessary to determine both what the purpose of the exercise is and what the outcome is likely to be, as according to Lindsay and Orton (2011: 89), 'the planned activities in a group should follow logically from the aims and objectives of the group, which themselves derive from the identified unmet needs of the members'. In the past, groupwork traditionally, as highlighted by Brown (1994: 98), 'relied heavily on the use of discussion and a limited range of other activities. A much wider range of possibilities is now available ... and this is constantly being added to by the creativity of group workers and group members'. However, before you embark on any chosen activity, try to ensure that you are as comfortable and confident with the particular exercise as possible, or otherwise the group may pick up on any ambivalence on your part, question your ability, or not feel confident in the task themselves.

At this stage of the group the activities can take a variety of forms including, sculpting, writing, role plays, trust, relaxation or visualisation exercises, recording of themselves or others, DVDs and video clips. In addition you could introduce activities into the group via 'homework' or exercises between sessions, where members are expected to complete a piece of work which they subsequently share with members at the following session. However, this form of exercise needs to be carefully considered before introducing it, as it may invoke reminders of school for some members, along with a fear of further failure and humiliation; as well as the real possibility that not everyone will complete the task, and the consequences of this for the group.

When moving into the 'core phase' of the group it is important to think about the interventions you might want to use that are specific to this stage of the group. These for instance may be to highlight a particular behaviour, alert the group to something that hasn't been seen or recognised by the members, or confront a specific difficulty that has arisen. In considering such interventions the leader needs to be fully aware of the real and perceived power that they hold in the eyes of group members. Therefore the leader needs to develop a curious and tentative approach rather than a dogmatic one, with interventions designed to help the group go deeper and explore issues further. All interventions should seek to place new interpretations and meanings on behaviours, difficulties and issues. The timing of such interventions is crucial and not as straightforward as you might think, as to intervene too soon may risk missing the point and too late may risk someone being hurt or withdrawing. The dilemma faced by the leader in this respect is captured by Whitaker (1992: 288) who states 'which interventions will be useful depends very much on how they are made and on their timing, that is, the individual and group circumstances under which they are introduced'.

As has been stated previously, the purpose of your group in the core phase will dictate the overall direction of travel, but planning the content of sessions will require you to use the chosen activities, exercises and interventions to move both individual members and the group forward towards their designated goals. In essence you need to further explore with the group, issues, difficulties and themes as they arise, whilst considering the purpose and timing of everything you undertake within the sessions.

GROUP STAGES

What happens during sessions is important, so in order to help you better understand the life or path that the group may take, we are now moving on to consider theories and models of groups, both to outline these processes and to compare and contrast some of these ideas.

Although there are a range of models (discussed fully in Chapter 3) that help to explain the workings of groups, probably one of the most well known is devised by Tuckman (1965: 384–99) who identified five stages that groups typically go through in the course of their life and are referred to as forming, storming, norming, performing and adjourning/mourning. According to Price and Price (2013: 144–5) the term 'forming is the initial coming together of a group, any group, where the criteria for membership and the purpose of the group are known'. The conversations that occur may largely consist of safe topics that keep the individual protected within the group. The second stage 'storming is when the group begins to sort out behavioural roles and individuals within the group begin to find what their place in the pecking order is'. It can be punctuated by power struggles, arguments and testing out, or equally with a co-operative and far less traumatic process. The third stage 'norming is a time when the group has formed an idea of who is who and is accepting of the reality of the situation' with functional roles decided upon and rituals and procedures agreed. At this point 'the group begins to function less as a group of individuals and more as a collective body, where members consciously or unconsciously accept their roles and the function of the group'. The fourth stage 'performing is the time when the group begins to achieve the set task' and 'appears to be at its height in terms of problem solving by utilising the resources within the group'. This should mean that members are working well together and the arguments and testing out within the storming stage have diminished. The final stage 'adjourning/mourning is the point when the group's original reason for being a group has ended and the life of the group is officially finished'. This can be a difficult stage for some in the group, for although a number of individuals may be accepting the inevitable ending and involving themselves in final goodbye rituals, others could feasibly be acting out, becoming withdrawn or sad as the end of the group draws near.

The above developmental sequence is largely mirrored in Corey, Corey and Corey (2010: 131–284) where they identify the following four group stages:

Initial Stage: 'The central process during the initial stage of a group is orientation and exploration.'

Transition Stage: 'To move through this phase, members must be able to deal effectively with defensiveness and resistance, confront their fears and work through conflict and control issues.'

Working Stage: '... deeper exploration and an increased level of group cohesion are typical of the working stage of a group.'

Final Stage: 'The final stage in the life of a group is the time for members to consolidate their learning and develop strategies for transferring what they learned in the group to daily life.'

Finally Oded Manor (2000: 97–201) in his book, refers to the four phases of group development as having clear identities, namely:

- *Forming the group and the engagement phase*
- *Authority crisis and the empowerment phase*
- *Intimacy crisis and the mutuality phase*
- *Separation crisis and the termination phase*

In summary then, the various models and theories identify similar patterns of group development, despite being labelled in slightly different ways. Whilst they all incorporate some different characteristics, the models each acknowledge in their description that the various stages are not necessarily followed in a linear way. Furthermore they suggest that with particular groups, some stages may not be reached at all, some stages may be visited several times and some may remain stuck at a single point.

Activity 6.1

How would you know, and what would you expect to see, when a group has moved into the 'performing' or 'working' stage of its life cycle?

COMMENT

As suggested a number of times in this chapter some groups can quickly move into this productive stage of the group where members are working co-operatively together to achieve the set tasks, and meet both individual and group goals, whereas other groups can take some time to reach this point in their life cycle.

CULTURAL ASPECTS OF GROUPS

The word 'culture' has a number of different aspects to it when applied to groups and its members. Firstly there is the culture that develops within any newly formed group, secondly the culture that individual members bring to that group, and lastly the impact that the organisational culture (and dynamics) in which the group is set, has on the group itself.

Identifying a group's culture requires you to ascertain what might be considered as 'normal' for that particular group. The members of any new group will initially join the group with their own ideas about what happens in the setting and who will be involved in the process. Then through the interactions that occur between members and the ensuing progress, the group slowly develops a culture of its own. According to Brown (1994: 92):

> Group culture is a rather intangible concept, but a very real one. The skill lies in establishing norms and a positive culture which is empowering for the members.

It is a fact that each member will have their own culture resulting from their particular upbringing, experiences and lifestyle, which to some degree the leader may have limited knowledge about prior to the group starting. However, how you choose to work with these members and their individual cultures within the group setting will be dependent on you and your style of leadership. Barnes, Ernst and Hyde (1999: 126) suggest that 'being in a group highlights the conflicts that everyone has about being the same and being different'. Each member then brings themselves to the group as a unique individual with their own sense of cultural identity. When referring to the dilemma faced by leaders in this regard Bergart, Simon and Doel (2012: 131–2) suggest 'they should appreciate and understand the differences among members and between members and the group worker, that may influence practice. Effective groupwork practice calls for cultural competence'.

Finally the impact of the organisational culture that has commissioned the group or where it is based, is something that cannot be ignored. This is best illustrated by the fact that you would expect a probation-led group for sex offenders with a mandatory attendance condition, to have a different feel and culture to that of a community-based support group for older people. Equally a group that is based in a building associated with a place of worship could potentially alienate certain members of a different religion or background. Therefore it is imperative to carefully consider what influence, if any, the setting and organisational culture may have on your group.

GROUP DYNAMICS

It is clearly important that when running any group you should have both a sense of 'group dynamics' (covered in Chapter 3) and the impact you, as leader, have upon them. According then to Price and Price (2013: 146), Burnes in his book *Managing Change* cites Cartwright as maintaining that 'group dynamics refers to the forces operating in groups and the study of them'. Another way of putting this is that group dynamics are the interactions which influence and shape individuals and their behaviour when brought together.

In the following paragraphs we will examine some specific areas that have a major impact upon the dynamics of all groups, namely: roles and behaviours; power; confrontation and challenge; scapegoating; collusion; silence; identifying and managing conflict.

Roles and behaviours

According to Whitaker (1992: 43), 'when a person first enters a group, he or she can be expected to seek a position in the group which is familiar and feels safe'. They suggest that for some people this will immediately mean seeking a position 'of power and influence' making both themselves and their views known to others. However, others will seek a more 'peripheral position' within the group 'and only feel comfortable if allowed to occupy it'. There are times where members, once they feel safer in the group, will shift or adjust their positions, whilst others will remain stuck in particular positions or roles for the duration.

In any group you will find that individuals occupy a range of diverse roles and display a number of different types of behaviour. These are described in various ways by different authors, but most attention is given to those more problematic or difficult behaviours that as a leader you may encounter. It is likely regardless of whether you are experienced in working with groups or a complete novice that given sufficient time you could simply from your own experience of groups, groupings and teams, be able to name many of the different roles that individuals play within groupwork settings. Corey, Corey and Corey (2010: 196–209) list some of what they term 'problem behaviors and difficult group members' including those individuals who offer 'silence and lack of participation', which they suggest can constitute a problem for both the member and the group. They highlight that it is important not to chastise those quiet or silent members, but to encourage them by commenting on their non-verbal reactions and through use of the 'check in' and 'check out' described in Chapter 5, at the beginning and end of each session. The authors also describe 'monopolistic behaviour' where individuals are self-centred and talk a lot, needing to be challenged over time in order to avoid feelings of annoyance from other members. There are then the 'storytelling' individuals who use the group for self-disclosure and letting other members know about their life history, which again can divert the group from addressing the real issues. Other behaviours described include 'questioning', namely those who interrogate other members by continually asking questions and giving advice, and who tell others in the group what they should feel, do or indeed not do; interrupting other members by asking too many questions is as disruptive as constantly giving advice, when the member is in the process of expressing their thoughts and feelings.

Doel and Sawdon (1999: 179–89) suggest that 'when you lead a group it can feel like being dealt a hand of cards', with each of the cards representing an individual behaviour (of which they propose there are nine) that you may come across. They state that one difficulty is the tendency to see these behaviours as problematic from the groupworker's point of view, suggesting that 'the literature alerts us to monopolizers and deviant members, but rarely problem solvers and unifiers'. The nine possible behaviours they highlight include:

1. Monopolizing

    This is 'sometimes personified in groupwork literature as the dominant member' who takes over a significant amount of the group's time and speaks of themselves and their own issues; and prevents other members from contributing.

2. Leading From Within

    These are group members who 'exercise leadership qualities and functions', referred to as 'internal leadership'.

3. Challenging

    It is suggested that 'the very act of setting up a group and acting as its leader can evoke challenge' within the group. On occasions challenge can occur due to a 'perceived difference in role and power between the group member and groupworker' and/or could be related to 'testing what will be acceptable and what is beyond limits in the group'.

4. Keeping Silent

   The action of keeping silent is like 'no other behaviour in a group' and tends to 'cause such immediate consternation'. It is suggested that keeping silent can be seen as a powerful statement, but equally in a group setting may signify any number of emotions including 'intimacy', hostility, being 'switched off' or 'boredom'.

5. Gatekeeping

   This, it is suggested, refers to those group members who 'when the group gets close to something difficult ... might try to divert the discussion' by asking questions about another matter or raising something less controversial. There are times when respecting the 'gatekeeping behaviour' is appropriate, whereas on other occasions the leader needs to have the conviction to move the group on.

6. Joking

   When discussing difficult topics 'humour is the group's salt and pepper' and 'often makes palatable what would otherwise be unpalatable'. Although humour can be positive in being 'entertaining, amusing' and 'diverting', it can also, via the joker 'inhibit the group's progress'.

7. Being Different

   These members are those who are different 'throughout the life of the group' and 'are not able to modify their behaviour in relation to the rest' of the members.

8. Scapegoating

   This behaviour is where a 'collection of strong feelings of hostility are directed towards one person in the group on a regular basis by the other group members' and is dealt with in more detail below.

9. Blank ?

   This represents any other behaviours you may identify within the group setting.

Although group members are likely to perform most of the above roles uncon-sciously, it is important not to think of these roles as necessarily fixed as they can, as highlighted above, change over time. Indeed Manor (2000: 37–8) says that 'in order to cope better with certain roles, or to shed some, or to learn new ones – change is necessary. In groupwork such changes are pursued through enabling members to become more aware of their relationships: inside the group and also outside it'. The leader should also be cautious of giving particular labels to members, as these are descriptions of behaviours rather than of individuals, and can potentially impact on your interactions with them in the group setting.

Power

It is a fact that groupwork and power are intrinsically linked and you cannot mention the former without making reference to the latter when discussing group dynamics. This point is emphasised by Doel and Sawdon (1999: 13) when they state that 'for many different reasons and in many different ways, groups address issues of power head on. They are powerful in themselves; the power can be used for better or worse, it can be shared or withheld, but its potential and presence are undeniable'.

In order to consider who holds the power within a group we need to briefly look at the relative positions of the leader and the members. Firstly, if the leader is a social worker or another professional they will hold a degree of authority and power, directly resulting from their role. In some circumstances members may believe that the leader potentially has the power and ability, if they wish, to take some form of punitive action against them or their family. There is then the power the leader derives from being seen as the expert in groupwork terms, held within their knowledge of the forthcoming activities and exercises that members will undertake; to this effect they have the power to choose how much information to share or withhold from the members. If the group is being led by a single leader, rather than jointly with a co-facilitator, they will need to be careful to ensure that they do not abuse their power in leading the group and maintain anti-oppressive practice at all times; which is where their discussion concerning groupwork process with an experienced supervisor is crucial.

In some cases members will attend the group feeling oppressed, as a result of perhaps their compulsory attendance or lack of ability to influence the content and direction of the group. This can on occasions result in members seeking to exert power through their ability to challenge and confront the leader (discussed below), create conflict, frustrate and disrupt group processes, and through their attempts to divert or control the agenda, which can impact on the group in either a positive or negative way.

The power differential between the leader and members can best be addressed by an agreement to share roles and responsibilities where feasible, in terms of member involvement, in both the planning and delivery of the group. This is also clearly the case in self-directed groups where any power invested in the facilitator is eventually transferred to the members before they withdraw.

Challenge and confrontation

It is inevitable that in any dynamic group setting you will see some form of challenge and confrontation occurring, both within the group itself and towards its leader. Furthermore if challenge and confrontation doesn't exist within the setting then it is often a sign that the group is likely to remain static and unproductive. This point is emphasised by Corey, Corey and Corey (2010: 193) who suggest that '… people cease being effective catalysts to others' growth if they rarely challenge one another. If confrontations are presented in a caring respectful manner, these interventions often promote change'. Therefore, as leader, it is your responsibility to promote productive confrontation and challenge within the group.

Given then that challenge and confrontation is a usual and common form of communication, it is useful to explore what it is and indeed what it isn't, when it comes to groupwork.

Firstly it should be remembered that any challenge and confrontation that occurs is something that takes place both between members, and between the members and the group leader. It is also, according to Corey, Corey and Corey (2010: 193) something that is '... designed to help members make an honest assessment of themselves or to speak more about their own reactions'. In essence your intention when challenging or confronting is, according to Lindsay and Orton (2011: 48), 'to help the individual to raise their consciousness of some limiting attitude or behaviour of which they are relatively unaware, and to do this in a supportive way'. It is also important to note that confrontation and challenge is useful when it is culturally sensitive, appropriately timed and done without malice.

What it is not about is challenging or confronting the individual, but instead their behaviour or attitude. The intention of challenge and confrontation is not to embarrass, hurt, ridicule, or punish the particular member, nor purely to deflect attention away from yourself. It equally should not be undertaken in a hostile or aggressive manner. When a member confronts or challenges another individual they should not do so and then withdraw or retreat, thus preventing that individual from being able to respond or engage (should they want) in conversation with the member about what has been said, but should instead be open to seeing the matter through to its conclusion.

In the course of discussing Tuckman's work above, in relation to group stages, we highlighted that during the 'storming' phase, power struggles, arguments and testing can come to the fore. However, it is important to recognise that challenges and confrontation are something that can happen at all stages of the group, can be positive and negative in nature, and can often take the form of challenges to the leader. Corey, Corey and Corey (2010: 195) state 'though challenges may never be comfortable to the leader, it is important to recognize that these confrontations are often members' significant first steps toward testing the leader and thus becoming less dependent on the leader's approval'. It is therefore important for any leader facing a challenge within the group to model their response to members, in an open and honest way, without resorting to the need for defensiveness, and through treating individuals with respect. In responding to challenge and confrontation in this way the leader is therefore likely to enhance the trust levels within the group.

It is also worth noting that the manifestation of competition – that can include a pseudo form of sibling rivalry where individuals adopt familial roles – between members can also lead to challenge and confrontation within the group.

Case study

David was a facilitator at a residents support group and had one member who stated she was afraid of confrontation, being constantly worried that someone would challenge her about something that she had said. The member said this so often that it became a defence, leading to other members of the group becoming more and more wary about saying anything that could

(Continued)

(Continued)

be construed as a challenge to her. However, during one particular session the issue of honesty was being debated and so one individual decided to challenge the member about why she rarely contributed to the discussions and was so afraid of confrontation. She initially left the room, but with encouragement from David returned to the group and eventually disclosed that when with her previous partner, she had been the subject of domestic violence and had as a result developed an aversion to any form of confrontation.

Activity 6.2

What would you do if a member ran out of the room in response to a confrontation within the group?

COMMENT

In this scenario David was faced with an extremely difficult situation and chose to leave the rest of the group, in order to go and find the member. Whilst there is no right or wrong answer here, it could be argued that a better approach may have been for David to remain with the group, unless he thought she was in some immediate danger, and simply wait to see if she came back.

Scapegoating

The term 'scapegoating' is something that is widely used in today's society but Douglas (1995: 3–5) suggests that according to Maria Leach it has its origins in 'any material object, animal or bird or person on whom bad luck, diseases, misfortunes and sins of an individual or group are symbolically placed, and which is then turned loose, driven off with stones, cast into a river or the sea, etc., in the belief that it takes away with it all the evils placed upon it'.

Although within the group you are leading you may not see members being driven off with stones or cast into the river, it is extremely likely that you will witness to a greater or lesser degree an element of scapegoating going on. This appears for the most part to emanate from difference and is bound up according to Douglas in the complex notions of 'blame, prejudice, visible difference, intense dislike, frustration, displacement and maintenance'. The term scapegoating is further explained by Corey, Corey and Corey (2010: 78) when they state that 'occasionally an individual member may be singled out as the scapegoat of the group. Other group members "gang up" on this person making the member the focus of hostile and negative confrontation'. This is more likely to occur once the group is established, unless the group are already known to each other. It is mostly the case that the scapegoating of an individual by other group members is overt in nature, but can on occasions take a more subtle form.

Although you will not be the first leader to find the process of scapegoating both difficult and possibly distasteful, Doel and Sawdon (1999: 189) suggest that you should 'learn to treat behaviours in the group as messages rather than problems'. They suggest that scapegoating behaviours should be regarded not as 'dysfunctional problems but as communications to the group members and workers, capable of helping or hindering the group's work, and sometimes both at the same time'.

It is without doubt difficult to manage scapegoating within a group setting, unless the leader is firstly able to recognise and then acknowledge in front of members that it is occurring. However this process is made somewhat easier if in the first session when the group deals with 'ground rules' they include the need to treat other members with 'respect' and are given permission to challenge discriminatory words or actions of others. Through acknowledging that scapegoating is occurring then you can help individual members to take responsibility for their own behaviour and provide the group with the opportunity to problem solve. Lindsay and Orton (2011: 111–14) remind us that that when difficulties, such as scapegoating, arise within a group it is useful to ask yourself a number of specific questions, including whether what is occurring is a problem or an opportunity? Although scapegoating can be a problem, it does also provide the opportunity to have a useful discussion with members about the issue. If it is perceived as a problem, the question then is, a 'problem for whom? What is seen as a big problem by the groupworker may not necessarily be a problem for anyone else'. The authors go on to suggest that Brown (1994) provides possible responses to these difficult situations which include the options of:

- '**Do nothing** – It is a good idea to wait a little while before making any intervention, provided no one is being hurt. ... Learn to wait, watch and listen...'
- '**Indirect approaches** – The worker does not confront the situation directly, or indeed mention that there is a difficulty, but finds an indirect way of dealing with the problem.'
- '**Direct approaches** – Direct approaches involve making explicit reference to the problem.' This includes the options of speaking 'directly to the individual at the centre of the problem ... to the rest of the group ... or the group as a whole.'

Case study

Lynne and a colleague were running a local authority parenting support group for lone parents with members attending weekly 2-hour sessions for ten weeks. The group was running with parents who had for the most part been nominated to attend by professionals and was on this occasion made up of eight women. The initial sessions of the group passed without incident and all members appeared to be engaged and getting on well. However, at session three it became evident to Lynne that something had changed and there was some degree of hostility from a few of the women towards another member, for what appeared to be no apparent reason. In the following session the hostility got worse and despite Lynne's best efforts no one was prepared to discuss what was going on.

Activity 6.3

If faced with the above scapegoating what actions would you take as leader to address the situation?

COMMENT

What Lynne actually did was speak to the member being scapegoated after the group session, in order to try and ascertain what was actually happening to her. It transpired that the member's 4-year-old son had been accused of throwing a stone in the direction of three other children, nearly hitting them; each child happened to have a mother who was a member of the group. The other children's mothers had confronted the scapegoated member outside the group and had felt that she had not taken responsibility, or shown enough remorse, for her son's actions. From the information, Lynne was able to take the matter forward and resolve the situation.

Collusion

The term 'collusion' is used to refer to either the conscious, but more often than not, unconscious agreement between a specific member and at least one other member within the group, to prevent or divert the process. It can take the form of disabling discussions due to a tacit or non-verbal agreement not to talk about a particular issue or matter in the group, and frequently results in an informal alliance forming between those members. When issues in relation to challenging themselves or others are raised by the leader, those members deliberately seek to continue discussing the previous or another less difficult area. They may also use humour in a defensive way with an unspoken agreement to laugh or joke if topics become too heavy or emotionally problematic for them. On other occasions 'collusion' within the group will occur as a result of the group unconsciously nominating one person within the group to be their mouthpiece for when difficult issues arise. This member will speak up on behalf of the group, without the rest having to express an opinion or take responsibility for what is said.

In considering collusion Thompson (2009: 141–2) states that 'in a classic text Berne (1968) describes various games that can develop in interpersonal interactions...' and these '... can act as a barrier to open and honest communication'.

Earlier in this chapter we looked at the various roles that members can take on within a group and we ultimately believe that such roles can only be adopted and maintained with the agreement of the rest of the group.

It is also important to note that it is equally possible for the group leader to be collusive in their interactions with members. An example of this would be a decision made by the leader not to pursue a particular decision or course of action within the group purely in order to avoid a challenge from a particular member or members, and as a result stay safe.

This leads us around to consider what actions you will need to take in order to address collusion when it is happening in a group that you are running. Firstly, as with most matters as leader you will need to recognise and be aware that collusion is taking place within the group. Secondly, according to Douglas (1991b: 179) you will need to take steps to make members aware of the collusion in order 'to enhance recognition of behaviour which is collusive so that members may have a more conscious control over their part ...' in the process.

Silence

In this section we will look at silence as a group dynamic in terms of where it might come from and what it might mean. The act of silence can be something communicated by the leader, the group as a whole or by one or more of the members. There are of course many different types of silence and according to Whitaker (1992: 257) these include '... thoughtful silences, uneasy silences, defensive silences, silences which are a communion of feelings in the face of some shared disaster, tense silences and so on'.

We will begin by considering the silence of the group leader in relation to where this may stem from and what it may convey to the group. As a group leader you will need to quickly identify whether you are someone who loathes silence or an individual who is comfortable and embraces it, as this may make a difference with regard to whether you will jump in too quickly to end a silence when it occurs or alternatively let it go on for too long. Whether as leader you engineer a silence or one occurs naturally, you need to be clear about what is the purpose of maintaining it, as unlike other members you have a responsibility for ensuring that all things undertaken in the group have a purpose and more generally for members' welfare. An option is for you to highlight to the group that you are aware that a silence has occurred and about why you did or did not intervene to end it. If there are long uncomfortable silences within the group setting, it is likely that members will be less willing to want to return for future sessions.

When silence occurs in a group situation it can mean a whole variety of things but often feels disorientating and maybe even punitive. The silence can emanate from the group as a whole or from one or more members in the group who spend the majority of the session in silence. It goes without saying that silence can be powerful and it can make the leader and other members of the group feel on edge or uncomfortable with what is happening. However, Preston-Shoot (1993: 106) suggests that ' ... silence is not always threatening or symbolic of resistance, disinterest and aggression. It may reflect positive developments. Therefore groupworkers should tune into the meaning of silence, into what is being communicated.'

If individual members are silent you will need to try and gain an understanding of why this is occurring, as they can sometimes be seen by other members as being difficult or problematic. However, a note of caution is raised by Corey, Corey and Corey (2010: 198) suggesting that 'group leaders need to avoid consistently calling on a silent member, for in this way they are relieved of the responsibility of initiating interactions. This can lead to resentment on behalf of the member who is silent and the rest of the group, as well as frustration on the part of the leader'. They highlight that whilst individual members should not be chastised for their silence, they should be invited to participate and if their silence is ongoing for any reason, the root of it explored.

Although we have talked about some of the difficulties that can occur with silence, in essence silence can be a productive and purposeful space in the group for members to think about an issue or to consider their position. However, as leader you need to understand the context of any silence, ensure that it does not go on for too long and is talked about openly within the group.

Case study

Paul was a groupworker who was working with a number of young people around the issue of confidence building. One 14-year-old young man had said very little at the first three group sessions and in fact nothing at all at the next two sessions, despite the other group members trying to encourage him to find his voice. However, the young man in question continued to attend the sessions, which Paul felt suggested that he was at least getting something positive from the process. At session six the young man spoke on a couple of occasions and finally in response to a question directly to him, managed to tell the group that he believed that he now understood where his silence emanated from. He explained that he had been brought up by his parents in a household of seven brothers and sisters, where he was the youngest child and believed that his silence came from the fact that at home his siblings often spoke for him.

Activity 6.4

In considering the above case study do you believe that Paul should have intervened earlier in an attempt to ascertain why the young man was maintaining a 'silence' in the group? If so how could he have gone about broaching the subject?

COMMENT

As suggested above it is important to understand the context of any silence and what you believe is being conveyed by it, to the group and to you. In this instance Paul felt that despite the young man's silence he was still engaged in the sessions by his non-verbal reactions to the activities that were undertaken. Therefore he took an active decision to allow the young man space with the belief that he would talk when he was ready and had something relevant to say.

In addition it was probably no coincidence that the young man was in a group with seven other young people, which mirrored his sibling group and therefore subsequently re-enacted his familial role and position.

Conflict

It could be argued that when attempting to bring any number of people together (especially if unknown to each other) for the purpose of forming a group, it is inevitable that a level of conflict between members will result. Whilst many groups will work well together and quickly build a level of trust with one another, others take a more alternative path which is punctuated with reoccurring issues of conflict. Whichever the case when conflict does occur it should not necessarily be seen as negative, for if worked through properly it can greatly assist the group in moving on and making progress towards its set goals.

In considering conflict Corey, Corey, and Corey (2010: 190–3) suggest that 'conflict is a difficult subject for some people to deal with, both in groups and in daily living' and that '…when there are conflicts within the group, the leader and the members sometimes want to avoid them rather than spending the time and effort necessary to work through them'. However, they stress that the avoidance of conflict in the long run can be more problematic for members than actually dealing with it appropriately in the first place.

When conflict occurs within the group it usually results from a difference of opinion, belief, insecurity, an issue of diversity or slights (real or perceived) to that member, their family or friends. It is also important to note that whilst some conflicts within the group will be open, others will be hidden and will need bringing out. As leader you will see the signs of the dispute emerging within group sessions and will need to take steps to establish the origin of the conflict. When you are dealing with a group where some or all members are already known to each other you may come across instances where they bring into the group unresolved issues from outside. In some cases this can lead to cliques or sub-groups being formed between members and the group being split during times of conflict.

In terms of conflict resolution, then, within groups, you will not be surprised to hear that there are no magic solutions, but nevertheless there are a number of pointers that can assist. Firstly, in order to address any conflict you need to both recognise that it is occurring and take some steps to manage or resolve it, rather than simply ignoring it. Secondly, it is useful to acknowledge to group members that as leader you are aware that a conflict is taking place and that you want to work with them to try and find a resolution to it. This can be achieved directly by giving a summary of what you perceive is happening between the members in the group and inviting both their and other members' comments. An alternative approach is to use exercises and activities, including possibly role play, to chart a specific conflict scenario and then to look with the group at different ways of resolving it; subsequently returning to the conflict between members to see if they can use what they have learned from the exercise or activity.

MISCELLANEOUS

Below are a collection of miscellaneous issues that support and relate to processes that are in motion for the leader and members at this stage of the group.

Self-awareness

Whilst we are dealing with the concept of self-awareness in this chapter due primarily to space, it should be noted that it is something that is relevant to leadership across all stages of group development.

The first question we need to ask ourselves with regard to self-awareness is what is it and do you require it in order to be able to lead a group effectively? In response to these questions Doel (2006: 112) maintains that 'self-awareness – recognising what we feel, when we feel it and how we deal with it – is essential for effective communication'. If this is the case then the possession of good self-awareness is something that would certainly aid all leaders and facilitators and indeed without it, they are unlikely to be able to help develop this in individual members. However, self-awareness should not be thought of as static but rather as dynamic in nature and something that is continually developing and being challenged as a result of both the groups you run and the other aspects of your life.

Whilst clearly it is not only social workers that possess self-awareness, Lindsay and Orton (2011: 43) do suggest that 'personal awareness is a core requirement for social workers and is also one of the essential elements of good facilitation'. If this is the case then this would suggest that all social workers have one of the key attributes required to be an effective groupwork leader or facilitator. They go on to state that it can be useful to think about three zones of awareness:

- 'Zone One: Attention out: focused on behaviour, beliefs and on the outside world.
- Zone Two: Attention in: focused on thoughts, feelings and sensations.
- Zone Three: Attention focused on fantasy'.

Furthermore they suggest that 'personal or self-awareness is the gradual and continuous process of noticing and exploring your zones with the intention of developing personal and interpersonal understanding in relation to others'.

It is suggested by some that being part of, or indeed leading, a group can be a useful environment for helping us to become more self-aware and this is explained by Johnson (2012: 54–5) when he highlights that 'groups experiencing conflict and intimacy develop greater awareness of self and self in relationship with others. This, in turn generates reflection, discussion and possibilities for change'. She suggests that once members begin to share with each other they are learning how to give and receive feedback more gracefully and develop empathy, kindness, challenges and a sense of camaraderie.

Whether you are a leader or a group member, self-awareness plays an essential part in helping you to understand who you are and what you feel. The groupwork process can help those involved to further develop their self-awareness, although this may be a gradual process and ultimately opens up the possibilities for change. The groupwork setting also provides the leader or facilitator with a unique opportunity to develop as a worker in an environment where they are challenged and have to regularly re-evaluate their own views, attitudes and beliefs.

Difference

According to Doel and Sawdon (1999: 52) 'groups are microcosms of the wider society, capable of amplifying and reinforcing oppression as well as challenging it'.

In any group you are running there will be a collection of individuals all of whom are different in a whole range of ways to one another and indeed to you. The difference can stem from age, gender, ethnicity, race, culture, religion, disability, sexuality or simply their upbringing and experiences. All of these issues potentially have an impact upon the group process and as leader you will need to have an awareness of the issues of diversity and difference. The reason that this is important explains Barnes, Ernst and Hyde (1999: 125) is that 'being in a group highlights the conflicts that everyone has about being the same and being different' and that 'group members also need to be able to explore their differences in the knowledge that there will be no active reprisals'. They suggest that whilst it can be a difficult and painful process for individual members to look at differences between themselves, it is important to understand the origin of such differences.

As a consequence it is vital that, from the beginning of the planning stage, you begin to think about potential differences that members may bring to a group experience. This can assist you as leader in being able to predict and prepare for some of the more obvious differences that may surface in the life of the group, around age or gender, whilst others will be perhaps more hidden in terms of disability or sexual orientation. Whatever the case you need to be prepared to explore difference within the group where and when it occurs, in an attempt to help members obtain a greater understanding of each other's positions and experiences. However, managing differences within groups may not always be as straightforward as it first appears, as highlighted by Doel and Sawdon (1999: 51) in that 'themes of inclusion and exclusion will always be present in groups' and to make them explicit they will need to be introduced as a topic. It is worth noting then that exploring any kind of difference can at times result in conflict and, if not managed well, potentially oppressive experiences for some members. Therefore as leader you need to be acting in an anti-oppressive way in your groupwork practice and 'take account of issues of power and oppression at every point in the delivery of a group from its inception to its completion'.

Supervision

Firstly we are going to explore the difference between line management and what constitutes supervision. Whilst both are necessary, they are totally different in nature with regard to groupwork, although on occasion line managers can (due to a variety of factors – not least financial constraint) act as group supervisors. It is likely that line managers will by definition have a responsibility for keeping tasks on track and be more concerned to ensure that any groupwork project is in keeping with '... the aims and objectives of the agency' (Lindsay and Orton, 2011: 37). Whilst this is important, supervision will have a more varied remit and ideally should not be constrained by particular agency alliances or responsibilities, freeing the supervisor to focus on the groupwork process itself.

Ideally your supervision should begin before the first meeting of the group, during the planning phase. This will give you both the opportunity to talk through any issues which are presenting themselves at this point and enables the supervisor to get a feel for the group, along with some of the key topics. The supervisor will also be able to pick up and help you deal with any matters you may be avoiding, not just at the beginning but throughout the life of the group. When you decide who you would like to work with as a supervisor you may also consider working in a group, as this provides additional support and lots of opportunities for parallel processes to aid your understanding of how group dynamics work. However, one of the drawbacks of identifying a supervisor is that it may be difficult to find an appropriately qualified and experienced individual. According to Wonnacott (2012: 64), 'this requires considerable skill in working with groups and too often supervisors have had very little opportunity to develop and hone their groupwork skills'.

In your initial discussions with your supervisor several things need to be covered, such as 'do the supervisor and leaders share a rationale about groupwork and a theoretical framework?' (Preston-Shoot, 1993: 128–9). Preston-Shoot goes on to suggest that '...it is likely that different models and languages will lead to frustrated communication and to a failure to bring practice and theory together'. This need not necessarily be the case, however, as initial discussions should identify where further conversations need to be had.

It can be argued that in order to present a coherent picture of what is happening in the group and receive the most effective support, it is wise to keep notes or a journal recorded immediately after each session, and to create opportunities to add to the notes as thoughts occur to you during the week. Barnes, Ernst and Hyde (1999: 175) state that 'notes should include seating positions, absences (with and without apologies), lateness, a sequence of main interactions (including those on which the sessions opened and closed) and a summary of the main overt and covert themes'.

If there are two of you co-leading the group, thought needs to be given to whether each of you has a separate supervisor or not. Should this be the case then you will need to consider how best to amalgamate your ideas from each session, in order to keep each other informed with regard to your perspectives, feelings and ways of working.

Although this text is primarily aimed at people who are thinking about running, or are in the process of starting to run, a group, do not be fooled into thinking that once you have gained experience that supervision is no longer necessary; for according to Preston-Shoot (1993: 120) 'even for experienced groupworkers there is value in having a supervisor'. However, the authors would go even further and suggest that good supervision is always an important component of keeping practice alive and not falling into bad habits.

Activity 6.5

What might you look for in a supervisor?

COMMENT

It is likely that some of the things that you will be looking for from a supervisor will be someone who creates a space where you can take all of your concerns, worries and successes from your groupwork practice.

Themes

Another useful way of planning for supervision is to consider what themes the group may be working on, albeit unconsciously. These will emerge in addition to any given topic or agenda item being addressed and are often common threads that may include themes like loss, food, insecurity, power, racism, jealousy, etc. It is often at the point you write up the session notes and include some of the speech that members have used in the group that the themes emerge. In fact Manor (2000: 58) suggests that '...the worker can go back to the words group members have used, and ask herself: What do they all have in common?'. These commonalities will consequently give you clues as to the theme that is present within the group. On occasions the themes are hidden and there are concerted efforts made to avoid them, but nevertheless they will be present, and can give you greater insight into not just each individual's concerns and fears, but also into the group's own personality.

CONCLUSION

In the course of this chapter we have considered how with the first session behind you the group moves on to the 'core phase' and begins to explore some of the behaviours, roles and dynamics that can subsequently play out. The chapter starts by reviewing some of the types of activities and exercises that you could use in the 'core phase', before considering the various stages of group development. We then learnt about the cultural aspects of groups, group dynamics and the roles and behaviours that can emerge within a groupwork setting. The chapter also highlights the issues of power, confrontation and challenge and scapegoating in the group, before considering further areas like collusion, silence and conflict. It then moves on to stress the importance of the leader or facilitator developing good self-awareness and being able to recognise difference within the group. The chapter concludes by further considering the value of supervision in groupwork practice and how you can recognise the themes that develop within the group.

Further reading

Belbin, Meredith R. (2010) *Team Roles at Work*. Oxford: Elsevier Ltd.
Although this book deals with team rather than group roles it provides a useful way of looking at how individuals operate in groups and deals with key issues around roles, difficult relationships, leadership and change.

Lindsay, T. and Orton, S. (2011) *Groupwork Practice in Social Work*. Exeter: Learning Matters Ltd.
This book, in chapter 8, provides a useful guide for practitioners in 'coping with those unexpected or unhelpful responses' when undertaking groupwork, detailing the types of difficulties that can occur. It subsequently provides leaders and facilitators with assistance in putting such problems into context and a range of approaches that can be utilised in tackling these issues.

7

CLOSURE AND ENDINGS – WHAT NEXT?

Chapter summary

In this chapter you will learn about

- endings
- inter- and intra-group processes
- outcomes and outputs
- recording
- evaluation
- reporting
- revisiting supervision, support and debriefing
- what next and signposting

Whilst there is no secret formula to setting up and running an effective group, it does, we believe, work best when it is preceded by good planning and delivered by experienced and skilful practitioners. However, that is not to say that those of you who are newly qualified or less experienced social workers should be deterred from getting involved in running groups (in fact, just the opposite), as there are ways to help compensate for your greenness by either co-working with a more experienced groupworker or having someone like this in a supervising role. Whatever the case it is equally important that the group starts solidly, successfully negotiates the middle sessions, and ends well; however, neglecting the ending is likely to prove costly to individual members and the leaders alike. A good analogy to further emphasise the point is that if a pilot were flying an aeroplane full of passengers, and managed to get the aircraft to successfully take off and then flew the plane to its destination, this would be of little use if he or she did not know to land it. This holds just as true in the realm of groupwork, for as a leader you need to know how to bring the group to an effective end that best meets both individual and group needs.

In the course of the last chapter you learnt about how to take the group through from the initial session into its working life or 'core phase'. The text contemplated the various types of activities and exercises to employ, group stages, and cultural aspects of groups, alongside how to recognise and respond to group dynamics and manage other important facets of the groupwork process. As a consequence we have now arrived at the point where we need to consider the importance of group endings in more detail, including how to plan for them and what it takes to deliver them effectively. Therefore in the following paragraphs we will be focussing specifically on group closure and endings, and the processes associated closely with them.

ENDINGS

As the end of the group approaches, a variety of behaviours and feelings may be displayed. It is inevitable that any group ending, like other endings experienced in life, can be difficult, joyous, sad or a relief when it's over, but the leader's task is to try and portray some of the ways these may be expressed. In common with the last few chapters we are going to focus on the ending of a group that has been together for a predetermined amount of time, with largely the same membership. However, just before we do so we want to draw your attention to other forms of endings that may occur before the designated time for ending the group.

In an ideal world endings would be anticipated, subsequently worked with and through, with a way of managing the consequences of the ending found. According to Rose (2008: 142), 'every life is a process of attaching and letting go. Whether it is to people, places, ideas, emotions or activities, the ebb and flow of engaging and detaching characterizes human experience' and so it is with group experience. As we have seen groups can manifest a whole set of different and complex interactions and it is one thing to deal with those as an individual but quite another to manage them in a group.

Doel and Sawdon (1999: 252–5) identify four different types of groups on a continuum that present a variety of challenges in how to approach an ending. The four are as follows:

A – group members start and finish together

B – group members start and finish one of a programme of groups together

C – individuals join and leave the group at different times

D – individuals join the group at different times and commonly departure is death.

We are going to use, and provide, examples of type A later in the text. Type D is an example of where the group is set up maybe specifically for people who are facing the end of their lives or at least certainly viewed as a group with an open-ended arrangement with people only leaving at some transitory point in their life. The transition may be their death, but it also may be at a point where they may be moving out of the immediate geographical area or into a facility that offers fulltime care and precludes them from attending etc.

Therefore in the first part of this section we will turn our attention to concentrate on group types B and C. It is in type B where people start and finish on a module or programme together and where this is a part of a much bigger group. An example of this may be if, on your social work degree or qualifying course, you are able to choose a module and in doing so you would then become part of a sub-set of people that you may not ordinarily work with. Type C is where people can join and leave the group at different times. This is usually predetermined and the tasks or time frames are clear at the outset. What then might these groups have in common and what might the issues be that we need to watch out for? In type B it is likely that members will have identification with the bigger group, so not only will boundaries be blurred but '…where group members have knowledge of each other outside the defined group, beginnings and endings are less sharp' (Doel and Sawdon, 1999: 254). In type C the life of the group is punctuated by the comings and goings of individuals and it is an interesting point as to whether the group is able to move to the performing stage that Tuckman identifies or whether they are always in the forming or storming stage; or, if performing is reached, it can only be for a short time. 'Special consideration needs to be given to how individuals who are leaving the group at different times are helped to say goodbye' according to Doel and Sawdon (1999: 254). It is necessary to consider here how you build in acknowledgement of the endings, and beginnings, for individuals, as it is inevitable that these will not go unnoticed whether spoken about or not. It is consequently important that you prepare the way for every new member to join the group and consider a leaving ritual when a member moves on. Of course it may not always be possible if people arrive or leave in a hurry; however, it is worth having those conversations to highlight the fact that each person will have an effect on the group dynamic.

On returning to type A where the intention is that the group starts together and ideally ends together, there may be times when one or more members of the group are not able to continue, or circumstances where the leader has to bow out for some reason. As with type C, consideration needs to be given as to how these endings will be dealt with. It may be that individuals are not in a position to say goodbye to the group for either a practical/physical reason or that emotionally they feel unable to do so. Whichever the case the member's departure needs to be recognised in the group and the resulting loss acknowledged. This gives everyone permission to identify their feelings and thoughts about the departure and allows them to, hopefully, express these in a way that is helpful.

As Chris Rose described earlier, life is a series of losses and endings, as well as gains and beginnings. Consequently by focussing on and managing endings in the group, this can provide experiences of more constructive ways of endings, and will ensure that members can take away and subsequently apply this learning to losses in their own lives.

We mentioned earlier in the book that the time frame for the group to end should be explicitly stated from the beginning. This may seem obvious but it never ceases to surprise us as how often people forget that not only the group will end, but also that the date is set and is mostly immovable. It may also seem negative and premature to talk about endings, especially when there can be an air of excitement or nervousness as this new group or project is in the process of starting. However, from experience it is always better that the framework for the ending is put in place at the beginning, as this provides the structure that we have talked about throughout this text. It is also helpful as the group moves through its trajectory that the ending is flagged up from time to time; not to a point where it takes over the focus of the group, but enough that people are left in no doubt that there is an end point. This will also enable people to address issues that they need or want to, knowing that there is a limit within the confines of the group as to how many opportunities there may be.

As the end approaches, individuals may adopt one of several stances as they begin to contemplate the final session. Benson (2001: 149) highlights that 'the ending of the group is an experience of separation and initiation, finishing and beginning which can speak to something real and deep in us'. It is likely that some people may approach the ending with resignation and others will relish it, wanting to move through it and on to the next project. Although some may avoid the ending, many will embrace it and use it as an opportunity to grow and learn. According to Rose (2008: 142–4), 'for some members, the ending presents an opportunity for intimacy that could not be realised earlier on in the group's life'. The author also suggests that whatever the approach, it is sure that 'every ending may carry the resonance of previous loss' (p. 144). As a consequence it is useful for you as leader to be mindful of what is happening for each member of the group as well as for the group as a whole, for as Rose suggests, the 'group member who falls ill right at the end ...' and misses it ' ... may, for example, be in the grip of more than a physiological virus' (p. 144). Rose (2008) also highlights that 'The member who retreats into non participation for the final phase chooses a different style, but is also trying to get to the end without doing the work of the ending'.

Preston-Shoot (1993: 115–16) maintains that the typical responses to the ending phase of a group include the following:

1. Denial
2. Regression
3. Expression of need
4. Recapitulation
5. Evaluation
6. Flight
7. Other – possibilities include expression of sadness, anger, closeness, satisfaction and proposals for the group to continue.

Whatever the path the individual, and indeed the group, takes in relation to the ending there is nevertheless a sense of anticipatory grieving present – similar to the process that someone awaiting a relative or close friend to die will go through – which will raise questions and issues that will need to be discussed and thought about. It is often during this phase, that Tuckman (1965) identifies as adjourning or mourning, that the conversation will turn to other losses and deaths that people have experienced in life, along with members questioning what they have gained from the group, what they did not achieve, and what they may regret. This evaluation process can provide enormous insight for each member, but in tandem with this their thoughts must now turn to how the actual ending will be marked. It is here that the group can come into its own, by making a decision about what they need and want to do, in order to mark this transition.

In our experience members have felt empowered to take charge of the ending and have used a creative part of themselves to recognise, mourn and celebrate the group's end. The end will often involve food of some kind, with maybe a cake or some snacks for the group to eat. On some occasions members have chosen pieces of music to share with the group, giving an insight into that seldom or never seen part of themselves. Other members have chosen poems or read stories that either they have written or are a favourite of theirs. It is usual for photographs to be taken as lasting mementos of the group, along with cards signed by all members, or occasionally a token gift of maybe a stone or crystal. We have also had members who have lit candles and sung songs, and as can be seen when it comes to the endings, it can provide the opportunity for individual members to be as creative as the group feels it needs to be.

Case study

Glen was the leader of a group and was approached at the penultimate session by Audrey who was one of the members. She informed Glen that she was not able to attend next week's final group session, as she was going to be a bridesmaid for a friend and had been invited to attend her hen night the following Friday evening. In response Glen asked Audrey to think very carefully about missing the ending of the group – which he viewed as extremely important – and specifically to consider the impact of her actions both for herself and the other group members. Glen initially feared the member was using the hen night as an excuse for missing the final session. However, Audrey did subsequently attend the following week, informing him that she had thought about what he had said and had decided to be there for the end of the group, informing her friends that she would join them later in the evening.

COMMENT

As illustrated above it is not always easy to address and work through an ending, which may be equally true for the leader as well as group members. However, an ending is a significant point in the groupwork process and can leave a lasting legacy on all involved if done well.

INTER- AND INTRA-GROUP PROCESS

When it comes to review and evaluation it is important to understand that processing in a group, as we have seen, can take various different forms and indeed some are easier to see and manage than others. Even if you are not able to identify processes easily, be assured that they are happening and it may be practice experience or vigilance that highlights what may be occurring, as according to Lindsay and Orton (2011: 81) 'with experience, you will learn to trust and use your own process responses, and be more able to use the information they give you to inform your facilitation and choice of intervention'.

Although in Chapter 6 we considered the difference between group process and content, we wanted briefly to explain two other processes that commonly take place within the realms of groupwork. As you begin to identify the processes in the group you will be able to bring them to members' attention and as a result move the group on and encourage them to deal with these issues. It is therefore not only helpful to identify, monitor, and discuss the process between members (Intra) within each group session, but also what issues are carried by members between sessions (Inter) and worked with to a conclusion or left without resolution.

Case study

In the first session Sophie had said quite forcefully that she didn't think that this group was going to suit her, as they were not the sort of people she was used to and didn't feel she would be able to open up in front of them. Whilst no one else in the group said anything initially, it was clear with a couple of people that the comment had made an impact. Although the content was compatibility and ultimately trust and safety, the process was still to be worked through and that meant the group considering what she had meant by the remark and discussing the impact that this had had on them. As the group progressed and the members got more confident, they all began to explore not only what the initial statement had meant but also what impact this had had on the rest of the group members.

COMMENT

This is an example of where the process is carried between the groups and ultimately discussed at a number of future sessions.

OUTCOMES AND OUTPUTS

When as leader you consider the review and evaluation process it is also worth being aware of group outcomes and outputs. Firstly we need to start by defining the difference between group outcomes and outputs to ensure that you can differentiate between them, and suggest that:

> Outcomes – refers to any change that has happened, in this case, as a result of the group experience. This can relate to changes in behaviour, attitude or emotional state.

> Output – on the other hand is primarily concerned with the tangible item that results from the group's activities. This could include such things as a booklet, an information leaflet or any other end product.

At the early stage of the group the leader and members set the goals in the course of the group contracting process and through the group experience these goals will be achieved as a result of changes in behaviour, attitude or emotional state. These will include goals for individual members but also goals for the group as a separate entity. According to Doel and Sawdon (1999: 126), 'although it is necessary for the group to develop common process goals concerning the way the group will go about its business (in terms of ground rules, confidentiality and the like), it is important to be mindful that people can be members of the same group yet hold different outcome goals'. It must also be recognised here that even though desirable outcomes may be recorded, the group may achieve some unintended outcomes such as the making of new friends, building a new community or learning to challenge.

How then can you measure whether the outcomes set have all been achieved, particularly when some of these will be monitored by the group member and others by the leader through their note-taking or during supervision? This is clearly difficult as not all outcomes will be recognisable or indeed recordable, and for others the time frame for the group will not be long enough.

For outputs it will be different as the product or article will have been produced (or not) and so in that sense they are by definition more measurable. However the authors sometimes feel that it can put too much pressure on the group and the leader, to constantly work in a culture where measurable outcomes are the norm. Lindsay and Orton (2011: 85) state that 'partly it has come about as a result of an "outcome culture", which demands named, measurable and accredited programmes rather than those that allow the more bespoke process driven approach'. Therefore Manor's (2000: 35) idea of '…the painstaking work of relating specifically group processes to the desired outcomes' may be too pressured for most groupworkers to consider and indeed for most, a step too far.

Case study

Amy had been part of a support group for six months. The members were all trying to build up their self-esteem to the point where they would be able to take something back to a shop if the item should prove faulty, which at that point was more than any member had achieved. When Amy was sold a purse that had a faulty zip, she had the opportunity to return the goods. She

(Continued)

(Continued)

subsequently gathered the receipt, along with the purse, and returned it to her shop, presenting it in a way that was not angry or apologetic, and obtained her money back. Amy was delighted and came back to the group the following week, saying that even though she had been nervous about the prospect of returning the purse she had accomplished a positive outcome. In addition to this, she felt her self-esteem had improved through the act itself and thus by returning the purse, she had in fact achieved not one, but two successful outcomes.

COMMENT

We must not forget that the group leader will also have achieved outcomes and maybe an output. Whether you are a beginner or a more experienced leader there will always be challenges and lessons to be learned that will constitute outcomes or an output in the form of an article or report.

RECORDING

We now return to the subject of recording, which has been mentioned in previous chapters as the task that most leaders and facilitators maintain they loathe, and can on occasions be heard quoting the old cliché that they came into social work to work with people and not sit in front of a computer all day. Whilst acknowledging that this is possibly not the most exciting part of groupwork the authors maintain that the importance of effective and functional recording speaks for itself and as highlighted by Douglas (1991: 36), 'good observing may come to nothing if it is not well recorded'. In the process of writing up and recording each session there is often the opportunity for the groupworker to reflect upon what has taken place in the group and their part in the process, which can provide benefits at a number of different levels. However when the group comes to an end, the recording undertaken takes on a new significance in assisting with the review and evaluation process against individual and group outcomes, as well as acting as a tool for member feedback, a debriefing aide and can prove useful in reporting back to commissioners and other bodies.

In considering the importance of groupwork recording Preston-Shoot (1993: 44) maintains that it essentially has three main functions and these are 'Firstly to describe what has occurred in each session and the group overall. Secondly to provide data for evaluation. Thirdly to note significant events as a basis for discussion between workers, for planning future sessions and for discussion with a supervisor'. However, Lindsay and Orton (2011: 121) suggest the purpose of keeping good and clear records in this setting is more complex and go on to provide a summary of reasons for doing so, namely 'reporting to colleagues and management ... to inform and convince them of the value of groupwork, ... providing information for yourselves and your colleagues... about individuals' participation..., providing feedback to group members, keeping a record for yourself about group progress in order to develop your own skills and to improve potential benefits to the group, providing information for post group review', and 'providing information for formal research and evaluation'.

There are a number of different ways that you may have decided to record the group sessions, from using traditional written records through to sound and video recording. As you may imagine there are clearly both advantages and disadvantages to all these different recording methods, as with paper you have to rely solely on your memory or that of any co-worker, of what transpired in the group, whilst with the other two methods you would need to seek the consent of the members to use them and you may have to spend a good deal of time searching them for a particular section you wish to record. It should also be noted that with sound and video recording, you would no doubt still need to produce some form of written record of the session, for record keeping purposes. As a consequence, for the purposes of the following text we will be focussing our attention on groupwork notes and recording in a written form.

Let us assume that the group is coming to an end and time has come to gather all of your written notes together in order to begin the evaluation and reporting processes. If you are the type of leader who was well organised, took the time to carefully plan what you intended to record following each session and maintained this discipline for the duration of the group, you will certainly have a relatively easy task in this respect. However, if you were someone who was tempted to skip certain aspects of the planning process, worry about what to record once the group was up and running and have only a handful of notes, you are likely to face a more significant challenge. It is hoped that your notes of each session will provide you with the basic information and data that you need in order to complete the various tasks of evaluation, feedback and reporting back to any commissioners or colleagues. According to Brown (1994: 195–6) this would mean recording the group process and content of each session under the following areas:

Basic data – date, venue, number of meeting, members, workers present/absent (...indicating seating positions can be useful)

Plan for session – as decided beforehand (perhaps referring to the group as a whole, individual members, workers)

Content – themes, activities, decisions

Process – group interactions (relationship emphasis)

Individuals – notes on each member's participation and progress

Workers – notes on worker/co-worker functioning

Summary – linking what happened to aims and future plans

The above provides some useful detail in terms of the areas you may have decided to include when you designed your group session record form during Activity 4.2

in Chapter 4. We have used Brown's format to create our own version of this form in relation to a young carers group and include the example below for you to see.

Young Carers Group

Session 1

Date: 07/05/14

Venue: Millennium View

Present: JP, SC, CP, AB, BC, RP, AK, JM, AM (Members) PA & SM (Co-Leaders)

Plan

- Welcome & Introductions
- Ice-Breaking (Fruit Salad)
- Hopes & Fears Exercise
- Break
- Getting to Know you Exercise
- Session Review/Close

Content

The intention of the group is to bring together these nine children and young people (young carers) with the intention of creating a safe space, where they can share their feelings, have time out from their caring responsibilities, have fun and access any formal and informal support they require. The first session involves a range of exercises and activities designed to help the young carers to get to know one another and is also about obtaining information from the members about what they may want to do in future sessions.

Process

It was noticeable that all nine members appeared understandably anxious and quiet when they first arrived, for approximately the first 30 minutes of the session, most members relying on BC (the first to introduce herself to the group) to do most of the talking. However, following the fruit salad warm-up game, which all members joined in (although JP initially needed some encouragement from SM to do so) with more and more vigour, as it progressed the group became more relaxed with each other.

However, in the later exercise 'Getting to know you' it was noticeable that RP and AK who know each other from school, were picking up on what the other was saying and disputing certain facts (in process terms it appears to be something they have brought into the group, rather than an internal process at this early stage) and so leaders will need to monitor.

Process continued

JP and SC have struck up an early friendship in the group, as have JM and AM and CP, AB & BC are also loosely grouped together.

Individual

JP – extremely quiet and shy in the group and initially reluctant to join in fruit salad game until encouraged by SM. However, at the break began talking with SC and was less anxious in the later part of the session, being able to share some personal information about his home circumstances and care of his mother.

SC – like most members at this first session she was a little shy and anxious about the group, but settled more quickly than some other members and by the end of the session was asking questions about other members' stories.

CP – youngest in the group at 11 years old and appeared a little overwhelmed by the older and physically larger members of the group. However, appeared to have settled okay and was able to talk with AB & BC at the break and they apparently shared some common but distant friends.

AB – is 12 years old and the second youngest in the group. She like most of the others was initially quiet and appeared anxious, but in the latter half of the session became very talkative and contributed well in asking questions of other members. However, although talkative did not disclose many personal details about herself or her family circumstances to the group.

BC – also told the group she was anxious, but appeared reassured and reasonably confident in her manner. She took pressure off other members by offering to introduce herself first and in the first half of the group was the member who made the most contribution. As described, she has a number of shared friends with CP & AB.

RP – initially quiet in the group and at the point of the warm up (Fruit Salad) exercise when he became more relaxed. From then on he began to interact well with other members, apart from some conflict with AK when he stated to her on two occasions "that's not true" in the course of AK telling how she had helped her mother after she broke her arm.

AK – settled into the group initially okay, although like others talked relatively little. However in the latter part of the group she began to talk openly about herself and the care she was providing her mother, until the above incident with RP. She responded by criticising him and disputing what he said.

JM – was quiet but appeared to be engaged in all the activities and exercises undertaken in the group. He joined in when presented with the opportunity by other members but was less vocal than some of the others.

AM – stated at the end of the session that she had been anxious about attending, but had really enjoyed the session and was looking forward to next week. She told the group although she felt guilty to leave her mother with their next door neighbour, it was nice to be out of the house without having to worry about her.

Workers

PA – took the lead with welcome to the group and introductions, but forgot, as agreed, to allow SM to introduce herself and doing for her. PA had to work hard to engage members in warm up exercise and this required SM to assist with one member to encourage them to join in. Handover to SM went well, although SM had to check in front of members during 'Getting to know you' exercise about a particular aspect of it. However overall leaders worked well together as a team responding encouraging group to maintain focus on the task.

Summary

This first session of the young carers group went well with the length and timing of the programme about right for the members, who after some initial anxieties contributed well. During session there was an element of conflict between two members that may have originated from their previous contact outside the group; this conflict will be monitored by the leaders. The group is at the early stage, but appear for the most part to be slowly getting to know each other with some initial alliances forming and are working co-operatively together. During the review stage of the session the group came up with a number of activities they would like to do in future sessions and so PA & SM will shape programme to incorporate these suggestions.

Figure 7.1

The above example details the first session of a young carers group and this along with the records from subsequent sessions will help you to build up a picture over time of themes and how both individual members and the group as a whole have progressed. The detailed notes could also provide the information if required for members to receive written feedback on each session, but in order to achieve this it would be necessary to design a separate short template containing information pertaining only to that particular individual.

In recording your notes at the end of each session it will be important to record the thoughts, wishes and feelings of all those people that are part of the group and also your responses.

Finally in this section we want you to consider another important area that is closely associated with recording, namely that of analysis. Once you have collected final information in respect of the group from session records, user feedback, etc., in order to evaluate it you will first need to analyse the material. This may not prove an easy task as whilst there will be some quantitative data, much of the information may be subjective or qualitative in nature.

EVALUATION

The process of evaluation is about making a judgement about the quality or value of a service or goods and could apply in this instance to all aspects of the groupwork process including individuals, the group and indeed the leaders themselves. However, when it comes to evaluation Brown (1994: 198) rightly reminds us that 'objective evaluation of groupwork effectiveness is difficult to achieve because of the complexity of variables and problems of accurate measurement'. Nevertheless evaluation can be done at a formal and informal level and, as highlighted in Chapter 4, the group leader really needs to begin planning for it from prior to the group's first session. It can also be something that is used throughout the life of the group and can assist with diagnosing problems or identifying areas for change.

Although in the social work profession the term evaluation is quite widely used, it can still mean a number of different things to different people and therefore it is worth thinking about the following questions when we consider it in relation to groupwork:

- **What** is the purpose of the evaluation?
- **Who** or what do we want to evaluate?
- **How** will the methods of evaluation/materials be selected and used?

What?

The purpose of the evaluation may originate from a number of different sources including wanting to convince the agency that has commissioned or contributed to the funding of the group, that it has achieved its set aims and objectives; which could necessitate a formal report being produced for senior managers. Especially in these days of austerity it is likely that any manager will want to see evidence that the group is being appropriately run, is meeting the needs of individual members/service users and remains within any agreed budget. The evaluation may also be used by the leaders in an attempt to convince managers to commission future groups or provide funding to permit the existing group to continue meeting in some or other format, with the aim of possibly becoming a self-directed group at a given point.

In other cases the purpose of the evaluation may be to enable a verbal or written report to go back to a nominating agency (with the member's consent) in order to highlight what they have done in the group and detail progress made. This may help the agency in talking further with the member to ensure that they are appropriately linked into other services that they may need.

There is then the need to evaluate the group in order to provide feedback to the individual members and the group as a whole. As is discussed later in this section this evaluation may entail an aspect of individual members providing their own of the group, leaders and process. It is often useful for members to receive feedback about any progress the group and they have made towards achieving aims and objectives, large and small.

It is likely, regardless of any requirements placed upon you, that as leader and/ or facilitator you will want to run an evaluation for your own purposes, in order to ascertain whether the group and indeed individual members have achieved the defined or set goals. This will also assist with the process of future group planning and development, knowing what worked well and less well within the group. In addition it would be useful to run a group evaluation from a professional development point of view in order to receive feedback from members about your performance within the groupwork process. This is something that you can utilise as a social worker towards your continuing professional development (CPD) requirements and will help demonstrate both your ability to reflect and the impact your work has upon the lives of service users.

Finally the other important reason for evaluation is for the purposes of research.

Who or what?

Although it may sound a simple task who or what you are evaluating is much more difficult to quantify than you may imagine.

However in terms of who, it is likely that any evaluation process that you undertake will be primarily focused on trying to measure the changes that have occurred with each individual member, as a direct result of the groupwork intervention, followed closely by those of the group as a whole. The evaluation will also inevitably produce information, whether directly or indirectly, in relation to leadership within the group.

In terms of what is being measured, this almost certainly relates to the amount of change that has occurred with individual members and the group; and is likely, for a range of reasons, to be problematic to quantify. The first and most obvious difficulty will be how you can evidence that any change that occurred with a particular member has happened as a direct result of the group process, rather than from something from outside, or indeed a change that would have occurred naturally in time. Secondly you can only measure change if you have set a target, outcome or goal that is SMART in nature, that is *Specific, Measurable, Achievable, Realistic* and *Timely*. However, the downside of making everything a SMART target is that you run the risk of measuring the wrong things. For instance, in groupwork evaluation terms the commissioning agency may be specifically interested in the level of member attendance (something that is easy to measure), which can be an indication of engagement in the group process, but does not necessarily indicate whether any beneficial change (which by definition is harder to measure) has occurred for those particular members. The difficulty of measuring change in a behaviour is further illustrated in the setting of a parents group where a mother may have an overall goal of improving her relationship with her eldest son, but as this is hard to quantify it is measured in terms of the amount of designated time she spends each week engaged in activities with him. Whilst the overall goal of improving the relationship is what you want the member to achieve, in order to measure it you may need to break things down into more measureable actions.

Finally the evaluation also needs to consider reviewing both the content and process, to ensure that all aspects of the group are taken into consideration.

How?

How the evaluation takes place will depend on whether this is a final evaluation, which is what we will be focussing upon, or one taking place mid-way through the group. It may be carried out in a formal or informal way and will involve the members and the leaders taking part.

How you evaluate the group will again be based on personal preference or the requirement of any reporting regime, but should start with a review of the individual and group, aims, objectives and goals that were set at or before the first session. As suggested it is possible to use a range of ways to evaluate the group including:

Feedback – during the final session it is possible to build in a formal evaluation and review with members of group content, process and leadership, in order to obtain their views. This can be obtained verbally during discussion or in writing asking them to complete an evaluation sheet on the day.

Video – as some members will be less willing to speak in front of others it is possible to set up a confidential video-type booth where members give their responses to set questions at the final session. It may also be the case that the whole session, or evaluation discussion, is captured (with consent of members) on video.

Evaluation Forms – members are sent evaluation forms in either hard copy or online to fill in after the group has concluded. The disadvantage with this type of evaluation is that it is likely you will not receive a 100% return from members, whose lives will inevitably have moved on from the group.

Questionnaire – as with evaluation forms, questionnaires can be sent out in either hard copy or online (possibly creating your own survey using an online template or format) after the conclusion of the group. An alternative is for the questionnaire to be filled in at a prear-ranged interview with the member, which is likely to result in a higher percentage rate of return.

Records – an analysis of the session records can often provide both quantitative and quali-tative data for evaluation purposes. This can also be used by leaders and facilitators to feedback to participants with regard to their progress in the group.

SWOT Analysis – another method of evaluation is using this form of analysis with either the group or individual member, to consider *strengths, weaknesses, opportunities and threats.*

Service-User Participation – although we have highlighted the importance of service-user participation in every aspect of a group's life from planning onwards, it is especially pertinent to mention it at the point of evaluation. Although it can be argued that many of the above aspects of evaluation including feedback, video, evaluation forms and ques-tionnaires, all involve members in this process, the concept of service-user participation requires a more integrated approach. When there is true service-user participation, the members involved will be central to planning how the evaluation of the group will take place. In addition once the evaluation is undertaken their views will be crucial to the pro-cess of understanding what worked well, what less so and what could be done differently in the future to make the group a more productive experience for all.

COMMENT

All of the above ways of evaluation have obvious advantages and disadvantages, and therefore you are likely to choose a combination of methods for your purpose. However our tip is to make sure you do build in space for evaluation at the final session, as there is a clear danger on being too reliant on obtaining feedback from members after the group has finished and risking the possibility of receiving little or no feedback at all. That said, if you are sending out evaluation forms post group to members, you need to decide what the best timing for the process is, to ensure members have had sufficient time to reflect on their experiences. If you are intent on ascertaining whether members have been able to sustain any positive changes resulting from the group, then you may need to complete a follow-up evaluation some months later.

REPORTING

Once the analysis and evaluation of the group are complete, it is likely that you will be required at some level to report back on the success or otherwise of the group. As a consequence you need to think about the audience for any report and the purposes it may be used for. Any report is likely to need to contain many of the following areas including, the dates the group ran between, the number of sessions and members (please remember not to use names for confidentiality reasons), attendance, aims and objectives of the group, the range of activities employed, feedback or comments from members, and the leader's summary, overview and recommendations.

REVISITING SUPERVISION, DEBRIEF AND SUPPORT

As we hope you have discovered throughout the book, it is extremely important to keep monitoring both your own and the group's progress; and this includes the progress of the individuals within the group. It is important to start with yourself as group leader, as 'being aware and coping with your own feelings, and recognizing and responding to emotion in the group, while conducting the group programme is far from easy' (Lindsay and Orton, 2011: 116). Regardless of whether you are running a group for the first time or are an experienced group leader, be assured that every group has its own identity with particular issues or foibles. Therefore, even after 20 years of facilitating and leading groups, it is rarely the case that we do not learn something new or find ourselves challenged by some particular aspect within group. That is what makes it exciting and rewarding, despite the obvious difficulties you will encounter.

What is certain is the importance of being supported and having someone to work through the process issues with you, and this leads us neatly to revisit the role that supervision can play in this respect. As has been mentioned in previous chapters, supervision is a really useful way of unpicking some of the knotty issues that may occur within the group. It is likely that you, as a social worker, will have your line manager as your supervisor (as discussed in the previous chapter) and whilst that is necessary and indeed often very useful, you may feel a little inhibited in talking to them about process issues; as they may have been responsible for agreeing to the group in the first instance and possibly the funding or other resources. However there are several ways this can be resolved if it is an issue. Lindsay and Orton (2011: 116–17) clearly define supervision as being located in line management and offer the possibility of mentorship (in addition to line management) for exploring problems or group dynamics. They feel that 'mentoring is about providing a forum for open exploration of the issues arising in the group' and this is necessary as 'groupwork is almost by definition more complex than one-to-one work, as there are so many more variables and you are engaged with so many more people'. Therefore, as an alternative to a line manager, mentoring can be provided by someone who is more experienced in groupwork and who can discuss the issues as they arise.

In an ideal world the possibility of a debriefing session after every group would be the perfect opportunity to discuss what has happened and what effect that has had on you, the group and the group members. This type of debrief could be useful when writing up your session or group notes.

If you feel that you would like to work with a mentor, then we would suggest you seek someone out who you feel comfortable to work with and who ideally has a lot more groupwork experience than you. Hopefully you will feel confident with them as the difference between mentor and supervisor according to Wonnacott (2012: 172) is that 'the mentor is not accountable for the practice of his colleague', however as part of their role they would discuss with you any issue that may need to be highlighted elsewhere. The other possibility is of supervision outside the organisation you work for and although independent supervision is likely to cost you money, it may be the best solution in some circumstances.

Whether working with a supervisor or a mentor it is likely that the basis for your discussion of group content and process will be based on your notes of each session providing an important record of the thoughts, wishes and feelings of both group members and leaders. This information will provide insights into what is working well in the group, what is not, and what you may be able to do differently in order to enable the group to become more productive. A discussion will need to take place about what exactly is in your gift or remit and what should be for the group to work on. For example the group may want you to address an area of conflict which they believe they cannot address, however it is more likely that if the group is able to find its own solution, in doing so it will feel more empowered.

Activity 7.1

Consider the pros and cons of having your own line manager as your supervisor.

COMMENT

We would suggest that when identifying a supervisor and/or mentor for yourself, in relation to the group, it is important to choose someone who is experienced, and you feel at ease with. However you must also be confident that they will provide you with the appropriate level of challenge and support.

WHAT NEXT?/SIGNPOSTING

In order to be able to signpost individual group members or indeed the group as a whole, to other support or advice systems, the group will be in the process of ending or indeed will already have ended.

However, there are occasions where you may have a clear and defined plan with members to end the group on a specific date, only to be faced with a decision as to whether to offer a further session. This may have arisen because there are one or two individuals who find it difficult to leave, that the whole group want to meet up again or that there is some unfinished business. Clearly this is a complicated issue as if you decide to offer another session you are only delaying the inevitable ending. Therefore if you decide, as leader, to offer a further a session this should not be done simply as an add-on or be seen as you bowing to the group's pressure; and the reason for your decision needs to be clearly communicated to the group. The additional session must then be planned, have a clear focus and be run on the understanding that this will indeed be the final group session.

Within the authors' experience, although we have rarely extended the life of a group, when this has happened, you can sometimes find that the session itself is not productive, even though it appeared to be providing a service that was needed; so our advice is to stay with the original date for the ending.

However, when you do finally approach the end of the group it is important to provide information about what other services or opportunities are available to fill the gap and/or take their development further. When you are setting up the group you will know what other resources are available in your locality and in the appropriate topic/subject area. Therefore it is useful to prepare this type of information well in advance for distribution to the group.

Finally it is not unusual that one of the ending behaviours that you may see is group members wishing to maintain contact with each other via the exchange of mobile phone numbers, email addresses and social media pages. They may ask you as leader, if you would like to keep in touch, so be sure you have an appropriate response to individual members or the group that conveys a clear message about professional boundaries without being hurtful.

CONCLUSION

This chapter has considered the importance of endings in relation to groups, as well as some of the areas that are closely associated with this phase of groupwork. We have explained the inter- and intra-group processes in relation to what goes on within, and what is carried between, group sessions. In addition we have looked at the difference between group outcomes and outputs and provided you with a detailed example of a groupwork session recording. We have explained the different ways in which an evaluation of the group can be carried out and how this can be used for subsequent reporting processes. The chapter has also re-emphasised the importance of supervision and support for the leader or facilitator, along with the benefits of an end of group debrief. Finally, we have discussed how to help service users and members to consider what comes after the group has ended and signpost them to other relevant services and resources.

Further reading

Brown, A. (1994) *Groupwork*. Aldershot: Ashgate Publishing Ltd.
In this chapter we have discussed the importance of effective recording of group sessions and more widely the life of the group. In his book, Alan Brown discusses the pros and cons of various groupwork recording methods and also offers examples of how it may be undertaken.

Lindsay, T. and Orton, S. (2011) *Groupwork Practice in Social Work*. Exeter: Learning Matters Ltd.
At various points in their book, Lindsay and Orton discuss the process of evaluation and its benefits. In chapter 9 they discuss how valuable it is to evaluate your own work and make suggestions on how to do this. Whilst this is specifically linked to the social work degree, the principles can be transferred to groupwork.

Rose, C. (2008) *The Personal Development Group*. London: Karnac Books Ltd.
Although not written specifically for social workers, Chris Rose's book has a good chapter on endings and their variable nature.

8

ENHANCING GROUPWORK PRACTICE

Chapter summary

In this chapter you will learn about

- a review of previous chapters
- values and ethics
- anti-oppressive practice and empowerment
- multi-agency and interprofessional working
- service-user participation
- para linguistics and body language
- reflective and reflexive practice
- professional and personal development

INTRODUCTION

In the course of the previous chapters we have explained what groupwork is and where it originated from, with reference to it being a form of social work intervention. We have outlined the host of theories, models and concepts that have played their part in the development of social work practice, and groupwork in particular. The planning and preparation necessary prior to the start of a group has been explained, along with the specific detail of how to manage the first session ('setting out') and subsequently progress the group through into the 'body of the work', covering the various aspects of group dynamics. Finally the book outlines how to successfully negotiate the end of group and help service users or members consider 'what next'?

It is perhaps then pertinent that in the last chapter we dealt with group endings, when we learnt that as the end of the group a number of processes come to the fore, for both individual members and the group as a whole. These commonly include a process of review (and reflection) in relation to what has taken place in the preceding sessions and an evaluation of the group content, process and leadership. The evaluation should assist individual members and the group to learn lessons from the experience and help them understand what issues need to be taken forward. Finally the members will hopefully have had the opportunity to express what they have learnt from the groupwork process, what they intend to do with it and how they will be putting this into practice in their own lives.

Therefore in this the concluding chapter of this book, we intend to mirror the ending of the group by focussing on the following three areas:

- review
- learning the lessons (key themes)
- putting the learning into practice

In so doing we believe that this will assist us in being able to revisit many of the key themes of the book highlighted in Chapter 1, including: values and ethics, anti-oppressive practice, empowerment – use of power; the development of practice skills and evidence-based practice; multi-agency and interprofessional practice, working with others in groups; the service-user experience and opportunity for participation in all processes of groupwork development; professional development, evaluation of practice, reflective and reflexive practice.

REVIEW

In the following paragraphs we provide a short summary of the previous chapters and will later consider in the evaluation what we have learned about groupwork from these summaries.

Chapter 1

In the course of Chapter 1 we began to look at the meaning of groupwork in terms of the challenges and opportunities that may arise within this setting. In so doing it was acknowledged that groupwork has, over a number of years, become an area of practice that is marginalised and seen as holding less value or importance than other aspects of social work practice. As a consequence the book sets out to raise the profile of groupwork through assisting the reader to build up their knowledge and skills in this area and to help social workers address their 'continuing professional development'. This is achieved through developing your groupwork skills against the nine domains of The Professional Capabilities Framework for Social Workers as defined by the College of Social Work, these are namely: professionalism; values and ethics; diversity; rights, justice and economic wellbeing; knowledge; critical reflection and analysis; intervention and skills; contexts and organisations; and professional leadership.

The chapter then moves on to begin exploring how to understand groups and groupwork, explaining that moving in and out of groups is both central and fundamental to all human activity, and uses an activity to get the reader to think about their experience of being a group member. It highlights that most groups that individuals work and learn with, as part of their studies, will have a special function of 'encouraging learning together with sharing knowledge, furthering understanding and the personal or professional development of participants as their common aims'.

There is mention of the fact that it is sometimes easy to assume that everyone understands the terminology used in relation to a particular area, when this is not always the case and as a consequence goes on to provide various definitions of the terms 'group' and 'groupwork'. Particular reference is made to the notion that groupwork, as a method of working with individuals, is something that is purposeful in nature and designed to facilitate a desired change, growth and/or development. It also points out that throughout the discussion on groupwork, mention is frequently made of the importance of key terms like interaction, communication and exchange between individual members, before going on to introduce the term 'group dynamics'.

The chapter concludes with a further activity designed to help the reader plan their learning and make notes of topics within the book that will be of most interest, as against areas they feel more confident with and in which they already possess good core knowledge and skills.

Chapter 2

In Chapter 2 we suggest that in order to understand contemporary practice and the context it operates within you need to have knowledge of how, when and why groupwork emerged as a recognised part of professional social work practice.

We begin by exploring social groupwork from its roots in the early 1920s in the USA and Canada, with its origins in the social gospel and settlement movements, which were closely aligned with religious, philanthropic and social ideals. It is noted that by the 1940s in the USA groupwork was established more formally as an integral part of the social work profession as well as a part of social work education. At this time groupwork was still in its infancy in the UK and was only just becoming perceived as a method of social work. However, in her pivotal report on Social Workers for the Ministry of Health in 1959, Eileen Younghusband promoted groupwork practice as an integral form of social work that could support individuals to develop in society and contribute in communities. So although there was a growing interest amongst social workers with regard to groupwork during the 1970s it was still in the early stages of development in the United Kingdom.

The chapter moves on to consider how groupwork has developed and become embedded in social work practice over many years. It looks at the structural, political and policy contexts of groupwork practice in social work, highlighting that groupwork as an intervention has been seen by some as having a low image. We stress that in recent years social work practice has progressively become driven by procedural and managerialist processes, resulting in it being focussed on values and objective quantitative outcomes measures (performance indicators) which in turn leads to a functional approach to practice that often devalues professional judgement, creativity and innovation.

There is then a consideration of the professional and organisational contexts of contemporary practice, defined by the standards, values and ethics through bodies like the Health and Care Professions Council (HCPC) or equivalent; as well as those contained in the Professional Capabilities Framework (PCF). We stress that the structural, political and policy environment of practice directly influences the organisational context of groupwork practice, which practitioners need to fully understand. In addition it is important to recognise that social workers also work in and with groups of colleagues from other professional disciplines and therefore need to effectively operate within multi-agency and interprofessional settings. This can provide an interesting perspective when we consider issues of power and power struggles in groups.

The chapter continues to consider the purposes and the limitations of groupwork as a form of social work intervention. It highlights that groupwork is seen as being goal directed, with clear purposes, goals and objectives for both the individual and group as a whole, with an emphasis on the power of shared experience. The focus then shifts to reflect on the types of group that exist according to purpose, namely the remedial, reciprocal and social goals models, which can be defined simply as 'helping individuals', 'helping each other' and 'helping the group'.

It was highlighted that in any group there are risks, to service users or members, of being stigmatised by labelling and stereotyping when members are linked with say a 'carers', 'bereavement' or 'mental health survivors' group. As a consequence groupworkers need to be continually mindful that service users may already be feeling they are disempowered and/or experiencing oppression, which will undoubtedly have an impact on the way they experience being in a group, highlighting that although groupwork has many strengths, purposes and possibilities, it is also important to be aware that it has limitations.

Chapter 3

This chapter begins by stressing that social workers 'must in order to be competent be able to use social work methods, theories and models to achieve change and development and improve life opportunities' (HCPC, 2012: 13 www.hpc-uk.org/publications/standards/index.asp?id=569). Therefore the text provides a brief overview of a number of theoretical perspectives and models, selected because they hold relevance for groupwork practice.

In the text we highlight theories that explain group development, behaviours and processes, known as descriptive theories. The descriptive theories can further our understanding of inter- and intra-group relations and more broadly group dynamics.

However, whilst helping to explain and predict behaviour they do not in themselves enable us to control the behaviour, only to observe and help participants to look at how those observations can help them grow and change.

The chapter then looks at theories that suggest that groups develop in a staged or sequential linear way, where the group moves through predictable stages, and refer to the overall development of the group over its life cycle. This starts with Tuckman's (1977) five-stage model of group development, and goes on to include a consideration of other models including Garland et al. (1965) who refer to the stages of: Pre-affiliation; Power and Control; Intimacy; Differentiation; and Separation and Termination. However, Gersick (1988) challenges the notion that groups progress in a predictable and gradual way through stages, suggesting that group development is characterised by 'punctuated equilibrium' meaning that it can be erratic and unpredictable. Other theories describe groups as moving through a circular or spiralling (upwards) process, as they develop, including Bion (1961) who came from a psychodynamic perspective when proposing a cyclic developmental model of groups.

The text moves on to consider systems theory and how this can be used by social workers to explain group processes and how groups develop, with regard to relationships, interactions between individuals, within and across different groups. The importance of boundaries is mentioned, which commonly defines who is a member and who cannot be a member of the group. Systems thinking argues that 'each system influences all others and is influenced by them' (Manor, 2000: 99). Kurt Lewin's (1947) 'Field Theory' has similarities to systems theory as it takes a holistic view of the individual group member and group environment.

The chapter moves from the descriptive to the prescriptive theories that explain group development and behaviour in groups. The four theories covered are:

- Psychodynamic theory for groupwork – this has been highly influential in social work over many decades and offers a broad perspective from a number of more specific models and theories, including attachment theory, initially developed by Freud (1856–1939).
- Cognitive-behavioural therapy – known as CBT has also had an important influence on social work practice, with its roots in psychology. There are three theoretical ideas that underpin CBT work and these are: classical (or respondent) conditioning – where behaviour is learnt, changed or modified; operant conditioning – where behaviour is learnt changed or modified through making associations between the behaviour and the consequence that results (reinforcement or punishment); and social learning – which develops classical and operant conditioning by including recognition of the influence of the person's thoughts and perceptions on their emotions and behaviour.
- Humanism and groupwork – has its roots in person-centred work and is about human experience and the individual achieving their potential.
- The empowerment model – has its roots in political movements and radical, critical theories about social change, supporting the development of self-directed and self-help groups; and is underpinned by systems thinking. It is often argued that groupwork focusses too much on changing something about the service user or member rather than the structures and institutions around them that cause them difficulty.

Chapter 4

In Chapter 4 we turn away from the theories that underpin groupwork practice to the planning and preparation required prior to setting up a group. We stress the importance of planning and preparation for the group and warn against the temptation of skipping this process or aspects of it.

The text then considers specific areas of preparation which as leader or facilitator you need to undertake, including: purpose; service-user participation; methodology; leadership versus facilitation; self-directed groups; practicalities; supervision; referral and recruitment; support; membership; content; contracting; endings; recording and evaluation.

We have suggested that in planning for any group it is important to be clear from the start about the purpose of your group, which is likely to arise from having identified a particular issue or set of circumstances that would benefit from a groupwork approach. The overarching purpose of the group then may be: remedial – to address their behaviour and explore their feelings; reciprocal – to gain social and emotional support; or social goals – to unite in order to achieve social action, change or development; or indeed some combination of these. In identifying the purpose of your group, you need to be sure that groupwork, which as already suggested has its limitations, is the right form of intervention or approach.

If the group proceeds you should then consider whether the service user/s will be involved in the planning, content design and delivery of the groupwork sessions. This could help to empower both the service user who is involved but ultimately other members of the group and indeed all of them if they are all involved.

We highlight that it is important in planning a group to have an understanding of the methodology you intend to use in your groupwork intervention with members, which links back to some of the theories we considered in Chapter 3. Having decided on your methodology you need to determine whether the group will have a leader or a facilitator, and in this section we explore the similarities and differences between the roles; including the benefits of the co-facilitator role. We also discuss self-directed groups, which require a particular type of facilitation, where the ultimate aim will be passing more power and control to the participants as the group progresses.

The chapter then considers that permissions may be required at the proposal stage from your employer, if a work-based group, or others, including parents when working with children. The need for a risk assessment to be undertaken can in some organisations be mandatory and can provide useful information; however it is stressed that risk is not something that is static and can both increase and decrease, throughout the lifetime of the group. Occasionally taking a risk can be beneficial to all. A key aspect of your pre-planning will be drawing up the aims and objectives of the group. There are no hard and fast rules when it comes to this but it is suggested that you ensure that what is proposed is both realistic and achievable; with no more than three to four aims and objectives in total.

We then considered whether the group should be open or closed, the size of the group in terms of members, where the venue for the group meetings would be and the length and frequency of sessions. In addition we thought about the need to offer transport and child care for members, the resources and funding required to run the group, and need for confidentiality within and outside the group. Finally we considered the process of communication, anti-discriminatory and anti-oppressive practice in its various forms (and what could be done to mitigate against it), information technology, supervision, referral and recruitment, support, membership, content, contracting, endings, and recording.

Chapter 5

In Chapter 5 of this book we move on to focus on the planning and preparation needed in order to set up a group, looking specifically at the practicalities of the first groupwork session.

We start by considering the setting up of the group in terms of the structure and plan for the first session, including the pros and cons of a refreshment break. The use of information technology is highlighted, along with the need to ensure that a balance is maintained between structured activity and unstructured or unscripted space for spontaneous development of the group; a list of the types of activities that can be used is provided. The setting-up phase emphasises the need for the leader or facilitator to ensure that the venue is set up before members arrive. There is also consideration given to the various leadership styles, theories and models that need to be considered by the leader, along with the various merits of leadership versus facilitation.

The first aspect of starting out is the welcome provided by the leader/facilitator prior to the start of the group, which is split into three areas, namely: greeting members with a smile when they first arrive; the significance of a welcoming environment; and finally the formal welcome to members at the start of the group. The 'opening statement', it is suggested, is a chance for you as leader to share with members why the group has been set up and what it seeks to achieve; or in other words its aims and objectives. We move on to highlight the process of member introductions in the group and suggest that some ways of introduction are better than others, and getting it right can prove a significant benefit in terms of helping to develop group cohesion at this early stage. Although members can be extremely nervous we highlight a number of activities and exercises that may help the introduction process, including: introduce your partner; my name is; and written names. There is then a need to cover the aims and objectives for the group and you will need to consider whether these are decided by the leader only (*low negotiability*), leader and members (*medium negotiability)* or by the members only (*high negotiability*).

The overall purpose of the group (e.g., improving parenting) will have been restated by the leader during the opening statement. Although the aims and objectives will usually flow from the purpose of the group, it needs to be recognised that they may change over the life of the group. The chapter also discusses the degree to which members are involved in shaping its content and direction. It is suggested that in order to have an understanding of what members expect to obtain from the group and what they are worried about, it is useful to run a 'hopes and fears' exercise with them.

The chapter then moves on to talk about the need to establish ground rules for members, via an exercise, in the first session, as they come with their own experiences of right and wrong, acceptable and unacceptable behaviour, which may or may not be consistent with others in the group. In the course of the first session an ice-breaking game or exercise is useful, designed to ease the tension in the room and promote interaction between members; suggested examples are given. The group then moves on to what we term the 'body of the work' where the group through discussion, exercises or activities makes a start on addressing the issues and reasons for them being there. Finally further consideration is given to how to record and evaluate the first and subsequent sessions.

Chapter 6

In the course of Chapter 6 we turn our attention to what we term as the working life or 'core phase' of the group. These matters were not covered in a linear chronological manner in this chapter as we needed to take a different approach in order to consider the important issues of group process and progress.

We began by highlighting that the groupwork task is made up of two distinct parts, namely the content and the process, and it is important for the leader to be able to recognise what is happening in terms of group process, which are effectively '.... patterns of behaviour which form in a group over a period of time...' (Doel, 2006: 59).

The chapter then explores content and process within groupwork settings in the following five areas, namely: activities and interventions; group stages; cultural aspects of groups; group dynamics; and miscellaneous.

When moving into the 'core phase' of the group we highlight that it is important to think about the activities and interventions you might want to use that are specific to this stage of the group. As suggested, these may be used to highlight a particular behaviour, alert the group to something that hasn't been seen or recognised by the members, or confront a specific difficulty that has arisen. The chosen activities, exercises and interventions are specifically designed to move both individual members and the group forward towards their designated goals.

The text then stresses the importance of workers having a good understanding of the range of models that help to explain the workings of groups. It subsequently highlights Tuckman's (1965) five stages that groups typically go through in the course of their life, which are referred to as forming, storming, norming, performing and adjourning/mourning. The chapter goes on to outline this and other models in more detail, highlighting that with particular groups, some stages may not be reached at all, some stages visited several times, and some groups remain stuck at a single point. Then we look at the cultural aspects of groups both in terms of the culture that develops within any newly formed group, the culture that individual members bring to that group, and lastly the impact that the organisational culture in which the group is set, has on the group itself.

We then move on to examine some specific areas that have a major impact on the dynamics of all groups, namely: roles and behaviours; power; confrontation and challenge; scapegoating; collusion; silence; identifying and managing conflict.

The roles and behaviours that members adopt within a group have been quantified in various ways, and include, according to Doel and Sawdon (1999), behaviours such as 'challenging', 'keeping silent' and 'joking'. Although group members are likely to perform most of the above roles unconsciously, it is important again not to think of these roles as necessarily fixed as they can, as highlighted above, change over time. It was stressed that, in terms of power (which can be shared), this can be held in varying degrees by the leader and members alike, although the latter can also feel oppressed within the group setting. It is inevitable that in any dynamic group setting you will see some form of challenge and confrontation occurring, both within the group itself (member to member) and towards its leader. Scapegoating is described by Corey, Corey and Corey (2010: 78) as occurring when '… an individual member may be singled out as the scapegoat of the group. Other group members "gang up" on this person making the member the focus of hostile and negative confrontation'. The text looks at possible responses to the manifestation of scapegoating in groups and what purpose it may serve for the group. Another common occurrence in groups is collusion when members consciously or unconsciously join together to prevent or divert the process; and it is stressed that leaders also have the ability to collude. It is stated that silence can be powerful and it can make the leader and other members of the group feel on edge or uncomfortable, however it can also provide a space to think so it must be considered both in context and as part of the dynamic. The chapter acknowledges that there is an inevitability that a level of conflict between members will result, when any group is formed. A good deal of self-awareness is necessary when dealing with any of these issues and indeed the chapter concludes by considering the concept of self-awareness and the differences in the group setting as the group progresses alongside the need for the leader to receive supervision, especially as these and other themes are likely to emerge.

Chapter 7

At the start of Chapter 7 we reiterated that in order to run a successful group there is no substitute for planning well and having some form of previous groupwork experience. Whilst there is no alternative to good planning, you can obtain groupwork experience by working with a more experienced colleague, or receiving supervision or mentorship from someone who is experienced in groupwork.

The major focus of this chapter was to recognise how important endings are with any group, including recognising all the behaviours, thoughts and feelings that accompany the end of the group. We recognised that life is a process of beginnings and endings and that a positive group experience could enable people to manage endings better in their own lives; some discussion is also given to recognising the many creative ways that people can mourn and celebrate the ending of a group.

Next we looked at not only the processes that happen in a group but also what happens between the group sessions as these provide vital pieces of information as to what might be happening in the group. These processes can also be responsible for outcomes – any change in a behaviour or attitude, for individuals or the group itself. Alongside this we considered the differences between outcomes and outputs and recognised that outputs are a physical product of a group, such as the leaflet.

Before moving on to evaluation we looked at recording group sessions and how that information can assist with the process of reviewing and evaluating the group. It was noted that there are several ways to be able to record the information, which can be in the traditional written paper form or via the use of technology such as video or sound recording equipment. The information recorded may also be required for a variety of purposes including producing a report, feeding back to the group, reporting back to a funding body and/or other involved organisation.

The chapter was also punctuated throughout with the importance of having service users involved in designing, shaping and evaluating the group.

It then made reference to the need for support for the leader in ways that feel appropriate, be they through mentorship, supervision or debriefing exercises; acknowledging that in order to provide an effective groupwork experience all or some of these need to be in place.

Finally, the text discussed the importance at the end of the group, of providing information that could signpost members on to other opportunities, experiences and support beyond the group, acting as a bridge back into their own lives.

LEARNING THE LESSONS (KEY THEMES)

In the course of this book we have learnt a number of lessons in regard to all aspects of groupwork history, theory and practice and now we want to spend a few moments in the final chapter highlighting some of the key themes covered in the text.

VALUES AND ETHICS

In the first chapter we heard that for any social worker who is considering setting up a group or is indeed in the process of doing so, there is a professional environment that they must operate within, under the Professional Capabilities Framework (PCF) and the Health Care Professionals Council (HCPC) proficiencies, which we discuss later in this chapter. This along with having an understanding of both where groupwork practice originated, and the various theories and models that underpin it, will hopefully help ensure that any potential leader has a sound value base and ethical stance with which to move forward. It is also important to acknowledge that your own values and ethics may not be shared by individuals within the group nor theirs with others members – which is something that could lead to potential difficulties in setting ground rules and conflict in later sessions. Although you do not need to be an expert to practice groupwork, you do need to demonstrate some core values and competencies, whereas groupwork experience can be gained in other ways, by, for instance, co-leading a group with another more experienced social worker or colleague from another discipline.

ANTI-OPPRESSIVE PRACTICE AND EMPOWERMENT

We have touched upon this area as a recurring theme in the book, highlighting that firstly service users or members may come into the group feeling as though they have been oppressed due to a range of factors in their own lives. In addition they may feel further oppressed if they have to attend the group as a requirement of an order, due to the expectation of a local authority or because it is a designated part of their educational course. We suggest that when a service user or member first enters the group they may feel a lack of control, that they have not been consulted about what is happening to them and that the leader holds a significant amount of power over them. They can also be oppressed if there has been a lack of consideration about any additional support, access (e.g., wheelchair ramps or lifts) or equipment that a member may require in order to attend and fully participate in the group.

As a consequence groupwork leaders and facilitators need to recognise the power they have (or are perceived to have) within the group and use it in a responsible way, reflecting upon the fact that where appropriate, power can be given up and shared with members. In leading the group it is important to work hard to ensure that service users and members feel empowered from their first meeting with you, prior to the group commencing, through to the group's end. This, we stress, is best achieved by ensuring that service users and members have a high level of user participation in the planning, design and delivery of the group itself. They can additionally be empowered by being provided with relevant information, being given choices and in setting their own goals for what they want to achieve from the groupwork experience.

We also want to briefly mention the importance of the leader or facilitator acting in an anti-discriminatory and anti-sectarian manner towards group members. We discussed anti-discriminatory behaviour in Chapter 4 and want to acknowledge that anti-sectarian behaviour means avoiding bigotry or hatred with regard to perceived differences such as political views, religion or class.

MULTI-AGENCY AND INTERPROFESSIONAL WORKING

As you are aware multi-agency working can involve several organisations who will come together to plan and deliver a groupwork service that is needed or wanted. In certain circumstances organisations or agencies may collaborate in order to provide input into sessions, as for instance with a parenting group (e.g., health visitor, police officer, nursery manager) on their particular area of expertise or specialism.

However, in interprofessional working individuals from different disciplines come together to organise and run a group, with the aim of working jointly in order to deliver the agreed set of aims and objectives. When this happens clarity is needed during the planning stage (and beyond) when it comes to professional overlaps and potential disputes that may occur in the delivery of the service. All professions and indeed professionals involved will have their own particular value bases and these in turn will impact on the process.

SERVICE-USER PARTICIPATION

We have previously stated that user participation in all aspects of groupwork process through the planning, delivery and evaluation stages of the group is an essential consideration for the leader or facilitator. As we have explained there are occasions with particular types of groups where this may be more difficult to achieve but should not be viewed as a reason to disregard it altogether, as in our opinion there are always opportunities, regardless of the circumstances, for some degree of service-user participation to be included. In the process of consulting service users and subsequently using their ideas, thoughts and views in the groupwork programme, we need to guard against the danger of simply paying lip service to service-user participation or undertaking it in a half-hearted way.

PARA LINGUISTICS AND BODY LANGUAGE

One area that we have neglected in the body of the text but needs highlighting and further thinking about, are the areas of para linguistics and body language. These important areas both need mentioning as other ways of providing information/clues as to what is happening between members of the group, what people may be thinking or in terms of what may be happening in the communication and/or relationships within the group. Para linguistics or para language is concerned with what happens alongside the words that are spoken, along with how the words are spoken. Body language is a part of this area and features things like gestures, facial expressions, the way someone sits but also the pitch and tone of voice. In addition there are the noises that accompany the words such as 'mmm', 'eh', 'aha', and 'oh', as well as sighing and gasping, etc., and these can be conveyed in various ways.

It is also important with body language (or body posture i.e., movements) to recognise and understand that there can be nuances and cultural differences in the way people present. Therefore it is important to acknowledge any differences and allow space to check out whether a group member's particular presentation has a cultural base and address any resulting difficulties or misunderstandings.

Finally, as a leader or facilitator you need to be aware of the way in which you present in terms of your behaviours and attitudes, including para linguistics and body language, as this will inevitably result in you modelling to individual members and the group as a whole.

Case study

Meg was in a group with nine others and the group had been progressing well. However when Eric, the group leader, suggested that they move on to talk about a more personal issue it was clear that Meg together with Josh, Masie, Gill, Jack and Richard were clearly uncomfortable although they all stated they were happy to go on with the conversation. However it was noted that they fidgeted and were constantly glancing over at each other looking for reassurance as it was discussed.

Activity 8.1

How might you encourage group members to discuss what needed to be discussed and also address the discomfort?

COMMENT

In the group proper Eric actually addressed the group's discomfort by stating that even though everyone had said they were happy to proceed with discussing the personal issue, it might be that some people were not. Therefore this allowed the issue to be named without singling people out and thus creating a space for people to acknowledge their position.

REFLECTIVE AND REFLEXIVE PRACTICE

In the first part of the book, particularly Chapter 3, we stressed the importance of understanding the part that reflective practice plays in working with groups. Reflective practice is concerned with how thinking through and considering the decisions made can influence future experiences of the group. For instance the first stage of reflective practice is to think about a situation or group dynamic that needs to change. We then need to think about the changes that are required to happen, plan the changes and subsequently move on to implementing those changes. For example, if when we are starting to lead a group, we use an introductory exercise that receives a mixed response, we should consider the exercise and the responses, thinking about why it might not have worked, and then plan what we are going to try to do next time and consider how we will incorporate the change into our programme. This reflection needs to be an ongoing process for all aspects of the group's life and can be recorded in your notes, shared in supervision sessions and learnt from for future work.

Reflexive practice on the other hand involves taking ' … a critical stance towards one's own cognitive and emotional processes…' (O'Sullivan, 2011: 10). This includes developing and sharpening your internal dialogue to further explore issues and ideas that you have influenced and those that have influenced you. In order to become a reflexive practitioner we need to have good self-awareness, which includes not only an awareness of ourselves and how people impact upon us but also how we impact on others.

Case study

Pat had led various groups throughout his six-year career to date. Whilst he had always been diligent about reflecting on each group's progress and keeping notes, he was challenged on one occasion by Alice, who suggested that he had made a sexist comment. This prompted him to reconsider his approach to working with women and really think about what had made someone assume that he had made this sort of comment. The interchange enabled him to re-evaluate his attitude and assumptions in order to grow and become more mindful of his responses. He was also able to further analyse the transference between them and gain a better understanding of what was happening.

COMMENT

Every interchange provides opportunities to gain self-awareness and therefore encourage personal growth.

PUTTING THE LEARNING INTO PRACTICE

Although there is an expectation for social workers to become involved in groups, and there are signs of a resurgence in groupwork practice, there is a danger that people may assume that it is a cheaper option when working with a set number of people, who on the face of it, seem to have a similar issue or problem. However, in some quarters, conversely, setting up and leading a group may be regarded as a luxury that a busy working week will not allow for. It is the authors' view that neither of these attitudes is healthy and it fails to recognise that groups can be and often are powerful experiences for members and produce a beneficial impact on people's lives.

In this final section of the book we will think about putting the learning into practice by focussing on your personal and professional development in relation to groupwork practice.

PROFESSIONAL DEVELOPMENT

We previously highlighted that as a social worker you work within a professional context and feel that it is important that we discuss this further, explaining how various aspects of groupwork practice fit into the PCF, HCPC Standards of Proficiency and Assessed and Supported Year in Employment (ASYE). However, we would also wish to acknowledge that whilst we are focussing on the above, we are aware that there will be social workers from other countries (within and outside the UK) not working to the PCF, as well as professionals from other disciplines, who can still utilise this book with its primary aim being to develop the groupwork skills and knowledge of the reader.

Professional Capabilities Framework (PCF)

The PCF provides an overarching structure for social worker career development from the point of entry onto their degree training course through to post qualifying and beyond. It is divided into nine levels of progression, along with nine domains of competence (that include a number of levels of development). We are aware that if you are a student social worker you are unlikely to be involved directly in leading or facilitating groupwork until at least your first placement; however you should still be able to observe group dynamics and indeed will be taking part in training and other group activities. The following are examples of the various PCF levels and the expected achievements:

1. Point of entry – demonstrates awareness of social context for social work practice, awareness of self, ability to develop rapport and potential to develop relevant knowledge, skills and values through professional training.
2. Prior to the first placement – assessment of readiness to practise basic communication skills, ability to engage with users, capacity to work as a member of an organisation, willingness to learn from feedback and supervision and demonstrate basic social work values, knowledge and skills in order to be able to make effective use of first practice placement.
3. By the end of the first placement – students should demonstrate effective use of knowledge, skills and commitment to core values in social work in a given setting. They will have demonstrated capacity to work with people and situations where there may not be simple clear-cut solutions.
4. By the end of the last placement/the completion of qualifying programmes – students should demonstrate an ability to work with a range of service users, the capacity to work with more complex situations and work more autonomously, whilst seeking appropriate support.
5. ASYE (see p. 162).
6. There are a further four levels which continue the social worker's career pathway and are namely: Social Worker; Experienced Social Worker; Advanced Practitioner; and Strategic Practitioner.

In order to progress through the nine PCF levels, social workers need to be able to demonstrate their competencies across the nine PCF domains that we first outlined in Chapter 1. We have consequently relisted the nine domains below and provide some examples of how groupwork may meet some of those expectations:

Professionalism – social workers 'should take responsibility for their practice, together with their learning and conduct'

In groupwork terms, the social worker should be ensuring that they treat individuals with respect, keep professional and personal boundaries, and act with integrity in their dealings with service users and members.

Values and ethics – social workers 'have an obligation to conduct themselves ethically and to engage in ethical decision making, including through partnership with people who use their services'

In groupwork terms the social workers need to have an understanding both of their own value base (self-awareness) and that of others within the group; and need to be aware of the potential conflicts that may arise as discussed in this chapter in Values and Ethics above.

Diversity – social workers need to understand that 'diversity is multi dimensional and includes race, disability, class, economic status, age, sexuality, gender and trans gender, faith and belief'

In groupwork terms social workers as leaders and facilitators need to be aware of the differences with each individual involved in the group, in order to understand where potential conflicts may arise and ensure they act in an anti-discriminatory way. If the social worker fails to recognise the difference this could lead to oppressive practice occurring towards individual service users or members.

Rights, justice and economic wellbeing – social workers need to 'recognise the fundamental principles of human rights and equality, and that these are protected in national and international law, conventions and policies. They ensure these principles underpin their practice'

In groupwork terms social workers can use the group as a vehicle for positive change in the lives of service users and members and need to actively seek to empower individuals and the group to make desired changes.

Knowledge – social workers need to 'know and use theories and methods of social work practice'

In groupwork terms social workers need to have a good working knowledge of groupwork models and theory.

Critical reflection and analysis – social workers need to possess 'knowledge about and apply the principles of critical thinking and reasoned discernment. They identify, distinguish, evaluate and integrate multiple sources of knowledge and evidence'

In groupwork terms social workers may achieve these through reflective and reflexive practice, keeping relevant notes, the evaluation process and utilising supervision. This could also require the social worker as leader or facilitator to quickly analyse situations that arise within the group that may require a responce during the session.

Intervention and skills – social workers need to 'enable effective relationships and are effective communicators, using appropriate skills. Using their professional judgement, they employ a range of interventions ...'

In groupwork terms social workers use groupwork as a form of social work intervention in its own right. The skills employed by any leader or facilitator within the group will include effective planning and preparation, recruitment, communication, observation, evaluation and recording.

Contexts and organisations – social workers need to be 'informed about, and proactively responsive to, the challenges and opportunities that come with changing social contexts and constructs'

In groupwork terms social workers need to identify and seek opportunities for setting up and running groups within their own agency or organisation and outside it, on a multi-agency and interprofessional basis. They will also need to be able to balance their roles and responsibilities, as part of the organisation they work for, as against those they have in relation to the group.

Professional leadership – 'the social work profession evolves through the contribution of its members in activities such as practice research, supervision, assessment of practice, teaching and management'

In groupwork terms social workers need to take responsibility for managing the preparation and planning of the group, in addition to their role as leader or facilitator. It is possible that through the process of running a group, the social worker in leading or facilitating the group may become part of a research study project.

Finally under the PCF Framework it should be noted that right from the beginning of a person's decision to apply for social work training, they will be expected to participate in groups, with some courses requiring the applicant to be involved in a group interview.

Case study

Alison was a student social worker in her third year of training. As her placement had progressed it had been agreed that she would take the lead with a group that she had been involved with for a few months. The group was made up of ten young mothers who were learning parenting skills and operated on a rolling programme during term times.

Activity 8.2

Which of the PCF domains would this experience cover?

Assessed and Supported Year in Employment (ASYE)

In the PCF domains above one of the key points in the development of a social worker will be during their first year after qualifying in their assessed and supported year in employment (ASYE). As a consequence we have taken the opportunity to highlight the PCF Framework requirements for the ASYE social workers and although you will note that undertaking groupwork practice is not specifically mentioned, it can, as outlined above, provide evidence to demonstrate your competencies across the nine domains.

As you gain more experience as a social worker, the PCF requirements increase and are set out in summary below:

- By the end of ASYE – students should have consistently demonstrated practice in a wider range of tasks and roles and gained more experience and skills in relation to particular setting and user group.
- In the social work role they progress to practise effectively, exercising higher quality judgements, in situations of increasing complexity, risk, uncertainty and challenge.
- Experienced social workers are more autonomous in their role. They demonstrate expert and effective practice in complex situations, assessing and managing high levels of risk.
- At advanced level, it is expected that all social workers will provide practice and/or professional leadership, through the development of research-informed practice.

Finally in this section we wanted to return to Activity 1.3 back in Chapter 1, which encouraged you to make a study plan for your own learning with regard to groupwork as a form of social work practice. Hopefully in undertaking this task you were able to increase your awareness concerning your own strengths, skills and knowledge in relation to groupwork theory and practice, identify your learning needs and the most effective way for you to address them in your continuing professional development (under the above PCF and in conjunction with the HCPC Standards of Proficiency). It would be useful then for you to review your study plan at the conclusion of this book to see what you have learnt and what learning needs still remain.

> ## Activity 8.3
>
> In relation to the above consider the following questions:
>
> - What part do you play in your team?
> - How effective do you believe your line manager/leader to be?
> - In multi-professional settings or meetings are there any professionals that seem to have more/less power, and if so why?

COMMENT

Given that a good deal of social work activities happen in a group or team setting, it is vital that social workers understand what can and does happen in a group. Although the book is set up with a view to leading a group, the concepts are equally relevant to other groups that you may be a part of or belong to.

PERSONAL DEVELOPMENT

Although the PCF and HCPC Standards of Proficiency will help to regulate your professional development, groupwork practice is also likely to have a significant impact on your personal development.

As a leader or facilitator you will want, as the group moves forward, to see that members grow and change, achieving most of their goals along the way. However as we mentioned earlier the group will also be a source of learning and personal development for you as group leader or facilitator. There will always be the obvious goals or achievements such as simply gaining groupwork experience, as well as improving your communication skills and competence in relation to planning, preparation and group endings. However, alongside these goals are the challenges and developments that you go through in tandem with the progress of the group and these help to enhance your abilities to respond to situations where you are faced with: sudden questions that you are expected to answer in respect to some aspect of group dynamics; personal questions you didn't want to answer; the first time you have someone walk out of a group because they are angry or upset; and the conversations that you are party to and don't have a fully formed idea of your opinion. All of these situations provide you with opportunities for your personal development and will be issues that should be discussed in supervision, and from which you can gain various degrees of learning.

We hope that this book will stimulate you into thinking about leading a group of your own and in these days of video calls/conferencing, it is possible to consider leading a virtual group, where individuals who wish to be part of the group can access the medium through platforms such as Skype and other forums. However, you need to be aware that generally video chatting programmes can at most only support up to ten people at a time with limited opportunities to observe the more subtle interactions such as body language. That said, for successful groupwork the authors feel there is no substitute for meeting members face-to-face where possible.

CONCLUSION

The final chapter takes time to review the previous seven chapters in order to remind you about what the book has covered in relation to the various aspects of groupwork theory and practice. The text then moves on to consider what lessons have been learned and in the process revisits some of the book's key themes, including anti-oppressive practice, empowerment, multi-agency and interprofessional working, as well as service-user participation. It also takes the opportunity to highlight two areas not previously mentioned, namely para linguistics and body language, and that of reflective and reflexive practice. The chapter concludes by looking at how groupwork practice relates to the various areas of your own personal and professional development.

FINAL THOUGHT

We hope that you have enjoyed this book, found it a useful reference source and as a consequence find yourself feeling more confident and enthusiastic about the prospects of identifying opportunities in the future to practise groupwork.

Further reading

Howe, D. (2008) *The Emotionally Intelligent Social Worker*. Basingstoke: Palgrave Macmillan.
As David Howe's book highlights, personal development for social workers is crucial. Emotional development is charted, whilst he advocates that social workers are more likely to be resilient, as well as effective, the more emotionally intelligent they become.

Howe, K. and Gray, I. (2013) *Effective Supervision in Social Work*. London: SAGE, Learning Matters.
In this book the authors discuss various aspect of reflection and how it is useful in relation to supervisory relationships. Chapter 5 is particularly helpful in understanding the necessary foundations for reflection and how it can be used within supervision.

The College of Social Work website – http//www.tcsw.org.uk/contact-us/
Health Care Professionals Council website – www..hpc-uk.org/
In order to consider the intricacies of the Professional Capabilities Framework and Standards of Proficiency, you will find it helpful to access both The College of Social Work website and the HCPC website. On these pages you will find the two sets of standards and how they are mapped against each other.

APPENDIX 1

THE COLLEGE OF SOCIAL WORK PROFESSIONAL CAPABILITIES FRAMEWORK

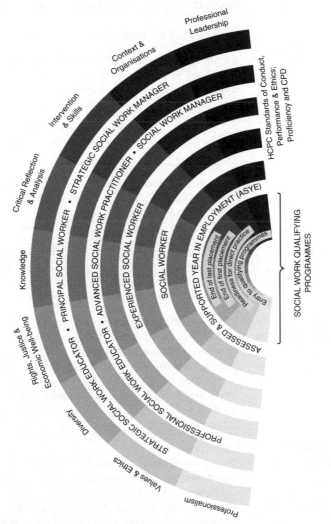

Figure A1 PCF fan diagram

© The College of Social Work

Accessed on 30th July 2014 and reproduced with the kind permission of The College of Social Work. Correct at time of going to press. The PCF is subject to regular updating.

GLOSSARY OF TERMS AND ABBREVIATIONS

AASWG – Association for the Advancement of Social Work with Groups

http://www.aaswg.org/
A division of the American Counselling Association, interested and specialises in groupwork.

ASYE

Assessed and Supported Year in Employment.

Group

A collection of connected or interdependent individuals, usually three or more people, who through interaction and developing relationships, work towards a common purpose.

Group dynamics

The active, fluid processes that take place in groups; how people react, interact, change and make decisions in groups.

Groupwork

The method, process, activity, or practice of working with groups of people who come together (either in person or by other means, such as virtually) in one or more sessions to facilitate a desired change, growth and/or development.

HCPC – Health and Care Professions Council

http://www.hpc-uk.org/ The HCPC are the regulating body for social work in England. They maintain a register of social workers who meet their standards for their training, professional skills, behaviour and health.

HCPC – SOPs Health and Care Professions Council Standards of Proficiency

The standards of proficiency (SOPs) set out what a social worker in England should know, understand and be able to do when they complete their social work training so that they can register with the HCPC. They set out clear expectations of a social worker's knowledge and abilities when they start practising. They are available to download from http://www.hpc-uk.org/publications/standards/index.asp?id=569

IASWG – International Association of Social Work with Groups

http://iaswg.org/
The International Association for Social Work with Groups is an American-based international association for social workers and allied helping professionals engaged in groupwork. IASWG seeks to promote excellence in groupwork practice, education, field instruction, research and publications.

IFSW – International Federation of Social Workers	http://ifsw.org/ The International Federation of Social Workers is a global organisation striving for social justice, human rights and social development through the promotion of social work, best practice models and the facilitation of international cooperation.
PCF Professional Capabilities Framework	The Professional Capabilities Framework is an overarching professional standards framework owned by The College of Social Work. It sets out consistent expectations of social workers in England at every stage in their career. Available from http://www.tcsw.org.uk/ProfessionalCapabilitiesFramework/
Quality Assurance Agency	www.qaa.ac.uk The Quality Assurance Agency for Higher Education (QAA) safeguards standards and enhances the quality of UK higher education.
SMART	SMART goals are generally used to mean that they are Specific, Measurable, Achievable, Realistic, Time-bound. The term was first used in the November 1981 paper by George T. Doran entitled 'There's a S.M.A.R.T. way to write management goals and objectives' published in *Management Review*.
SWOT Analysis	SWOT Analysis is a term used to refer to a way of considering the Strengths, Weaknesses, Opportunities and Threats of any project or business. It is a term credited to Albert Humphrey who led a research project in 1960s and 1970s using the data of various companies.
TCSW – The College of Social Work	www.collegeofsocialwork.org The College of Social Work is an independent, membership organisation providing practical tools and resources to its members to enable them to uphold and strengthen standards of professional practice. The College works within the regulatory framework for social work in England.

REFERENCES

Alle-Corliss, L. and Alle-Corliss, R. (2009) *Groupwork: A Practical Guide to Developing Groups in Agency Settings*. Hoboken, New Jersey: John Wiley and Sons.

Andrews, J. (2001) 'Group Work's Place in Social Work: A Historical Analysis', *Journal of Sociology and Social Welfare*, 28 (4): 45–65.

Bandura, A. (1977) *Social Learning Theory*. Englewood Cliffs, NJ: Prentice Hall.

Barnes, B., Ernst, S. and Hyde, K. (1999) *An Introduction to Groupwork*. Basingstoke: Palgrave Macmillan.

Bartolomeo, F. (2009) 'Group stages of development: Boston model', in A. Gitterman and R. Salmon (eds) *Encyclopedia of Social Work with Groups*. Abindgon, Oxon: Routledge, pp. 103–106.

Beckett, C. (2006) *Essential Theory for Social Work Practice*. London: Sage.

Belbin, Meredith R. (2010) *Team Roles at Work*. Oxford: Elsevier.

Benson, J. (2001) *Working More Creatively With Groups*. London: Routledge.

Benson, J. (2010) *Working More Creatively With Groups*. Abingdon, Oxon: Routledge.

Bergart, A., Simon, S. and Doel, M. (eds) (2012) *Group Work: Honoring Our Roots, Nurturing Our Growth*. London: Whiting and Birch.

Bion, W.R. (1961) *Experiences in Groups and other Papers*. London: Tavistock.

Birnbaum, M. L. and Cicchetti, A. (2005) 'A Model for Working with the Group Life Cycle in Each Group Session across the Life Span of the Group', *Groupwork*, 15 (3): 23–43.

Brandler, S. and Roman, C.P. (1999) *Group Work: Skills and Strategies for Effective Interventions* (2nd edn). Abingdon: Routledge.

Brown, A. (1994) *Groupwork* (3rd edn). Hampshire: Ashgate Publishing.

Carter, J. (2011) *Over 600 Icebreakers & Games*. London: Hope Books Ltd.

Children's Workforce Development Council (CWDC) (2010) *The Common Core of Skills and Knowledge*. Leeds: CWDC. Available at: www.cwdcouncil.org

Concise Oxford English Dictionary (2011). Oxford: Oxford University Press.

Corey, M.S., Corey, G. and Corey, C. (2010) *Groups: Process and Practice* (8th edn). Brooks/Cole.

Davies, B. (1975) *The Use of Groups in Social Work Practice*. London: Routledge and Kegan Paul Ltd.

Dearling, A. and Armstrong, H. (1994) *The New Youth Games Handbook*. Lyme Regis: Russell House Publishing Ltd.

Deasy, M. (2011) 'Groupwork with children from a disadvantaged community', *Groupwork*, 21 (2): 9–21.

Doel, M. (2006) *Using Groupwork*. London: Routledge.

Doel, M. and Sawdon, C. (1999) *The Essential Groupworker* (p. 117). London: Jessica Kingsley.

Dominelli, L. (2002) 'Values in critical practice: contested entities with enduring qualities', in R. Adams, L. Dominelli and M. Payne (eds) *Critical Practice in Social Work* (2nd edn). Basingstoke: Palgrave Macmillan, pp. 19–31.

Dominelli, L. (2004) *Social Work: Theory and Practice for a Changing Profession*. Cambridge: Polity Press.

Douglas, T. (1991a) *Common Groupwork Problems*. London: Routledge.

Douglas, T. (1991b) *Groupwork Practice*. London: Tavistock/Routledge.

Douglas, T. (1995) *Scapegoats Transferring Blame*. London: Routledge.

Douglas, T. (2000) *Basic Groupwork* (2nd edn). London: Routledge.

Elwyn, G., Greenhalgh, T. and Macfarlane, F. (2001) *Groups: A Guide to Small Groupwork in Healthcare, Management, Education and Research*. Abingdon: Radcliffe Medical Press Limited.

Fischer, J. and Gochros, H.L. (1975) *Planned Behaviour Change: Behaviour Modification in Social Work*. New York: Free Press.

Fleming, J. and Ward, D. (2013) 'Facilitation and groupwork tasks in self-directed groupwork', *Journal Groupwork*, vol. 23. London: Whiting and Birch.

Fook, J. (2012) *Social Work: A Critical Approach to Practice* (2nd edn). London: SAGE Publications.

Forsyth, D.R. (2010) *Group Dynamics* (5th edn). Belmont, CA: Wadsworth Publishing.

Garland, J. A., Jones, H.E. and Kolodny, R. (1965) 'A model for stages of development in social work groups', in S. Bernstein (ed.) *Explorations in Group Work*. University of Boston: Midford House, pp.12–13.

Garvin, C.D. (1997) *Contemporary Groupwork* (3rd edn). Boston: Allyn and Bacon.

Gersick, C. J. G. (1988) 'Time and Transition in Work Teams: Toward a New Model of Group Development', *The Academy of Management Journal*, 31 (1): 9–41.

Gitterman, A. and Salmon, R. (2009) 'Introduction', in A. Gitterman and R. Salmon (eds) *Encyclopedia of Social Work with Groups*. Abingdon, Oxon: Routledge. pp. xiv–xx.

Glassman, U. (2009) *Groupwork*. London: SAGE Publications.

Heap, K. (1977) *Group Theory for Social Workers: An Introduction*. Oxford: Pergamon Press Ltd.

Hedges, F. (2010) *Reflexivity in Therapeutic Practice*. London: Palgrave Macmillan.

Houston, G. (1993) *The Red Book of Groups*. Aylsham: M.F. Barnwell & Sons.

Howe, D. (1987) *An Introduction to Social Work Theory*. Aldershot: Ashgate.

Howe, D. (2008) *The Emotionally Intelligent Social Worker*. London: Palgrave Macmillan.

Howe, D. (2009) *A Brief Introduction to Social Work Theory*. Basingstoke: Palgrave Macmillan.

Howe, K. and Gray, I. (2013) *Effective Supervision in Social Work*. London: SAGE Publications.

Hudson, B.L. and McDonald, G. (1986) *Behavioural Social Work: An Introduction*. Basingstoke: Macmillan.

Hudson, R.E. (2009) 'Empowerment model', in A. Gitterman and R. Salmon (eds), *Encyclopedia of Social Work with Groups*. London: Routledge, pp. 47–50.

International Federation of Social Workers (2001) *Definition of Social Work*. Available at: http://ifsw.org/policies/definition-of-social-work

Johnson, A.H. (2012) 'The use of program and activities: purpose, planning and structure', in A.M. Bergart, S. R. Simon and M. Doel (eds) *Groupwork: Honouring Our Roots, Nurturing Our Growth*. London: Whiting and Birch.

Kindred, M. and Kindred, M. (2011) *Once Upon a Group: A Guide to Running and Participating in Successful Groups* (2nd edn). London: Jessica Kingsley.

Konopka, G. (1963) *Social Group Work: A Helping Process*. Englewood Cliffs, NJ: Prentice-Hall Inc.

Konopka, G. (1970) *Groupwork in the Institution: A Modern Challenge*. New York: Association Press.

Konopka, G. (1988) *Courage and Love*. Edina, MN: Beaver Pond Press.

Lawler J. and Bilson A. (2010) *Social Work Management and Leadership: Managing Complexity with Creativity*. London: Routledge.

Ledwith, M. (2011) *Community Development: A Critical Approach* (2nd edn). Bristol: The Policy Press.

Lewin, K. (1947) 'Frontiers in Group Dynamics: Concepts, Method and Reality in Social Sciences; Social Equilibria and Social Change', *Human Relations*, 1 (5): 5–41.

Lindsay, T. and Orton, S. (2011) *Groupwork Practice in Social Work*. Exeter: Learning Matters Ltd.

Magen, R. (2009) 'Cognitive-behavioral model', in A. Gitterman and R. Salmon (eds) *Encyclopedia of Social Work with Groups*. London: Routledge, pp.45–47.

Manor, O. (2000) *Choosing a Groupwork Approach*. London: Jessica Kingsley.

Manor, O. (2009) 'Systemic Approach' in A. Gitterman and R. Salmon (eds) *Encyclopedia of Social Work with Groups* Abingdon: Routledge, pp. 99–101.

Mantell, A. (ed.) (2013) *Skills for Social Work Practice*. Exeter: Learning Matters.

McCaughan, N. (1978a) 'Introduction: a framework for thinking about group work', in N. McCaughan (ed.), *Group Work: Learning and Practice*. London: Allen and Unwin. pp. 13–22.

McCaughan, N. (1978b) 'Continuing themes in social group work', in N. McCaughan (ed.), *Group Work: Learning and Practice*. London: Allen and Unwin. pp. 22–31.

Mullender, A. and Ward, D. (1991) *Self-Directed Groupwork*. London: Whiting and Birch.

Mulroy, E.A. (2011) 'Groupwork in context: organizational and community factors', in G.L. Greif and P.H. Ephross (eds) *Groupwork with Populations at Risk* (3rd edn). Oxford: Oxford University Press, pp. 446–58.

Northen, H. and Kurland, R. (2001) *Social Work with Groups* (3rd edn). New York: Columbia University Press.

Okitikpi, T. and Aymer, C. (2010) *Key Concepts in Anti-Discriminatory Social Work*. London: SAGE publications.

O'Sullivan, T. (2011) *Decision Making in Social Work* (2nd edn). London: Palgrave Macmillan.

Papell, C.L. (1997) 'Thinking about thinking about group work: thirty years later', *Social Work with Groups*, 20 (4): 5–17.

Payne, M. (2005) *Modern Social Work Theory* (3rd edn). Basingstoke: Palgrave Macmillan.

Payne, M. (2011) *Humanistic Social Work: Core Principles in Practice*. Basingstoke: Palgrave Macmillan.

Preston-Shoot, M. (1993) *Effective Groupwork*. Basingstoke: The Macmillan Press.

Preston-Shoot, M. (2004) 'Evidence: the final frontier? Star Trek, groupwork and the mission of change', *Groupwork*, 14 (3): 18–43.

Preston-Shoot, M. (2007) *Effective Groupwork* (2nd edn). Basingstoke: Palgrave Macmillan.

Price, M. and Price, B. (2013) 'Skills for group work', in A. Mantell (ed.) *Skills for Social Work Practice*. Exeter: Learning Matters. pp. 137–151.

Rose, C. (2008) *The Personal Development Group*. London: Karnac Books Ltd.

Schiller, L. (1997) 'Rethinking Stages of Development in Women's Groups: Implications for Practice', *Journal of Social Work with Groups*, 20 (3): 3–19.

Schutz, W.C. (1958) *FIRO: A Three Dimensional Theory of Interpersonal Behavior*. New York, NY: Holt, Rinehart, & Winston.

Shiller, L. Y. (2003) 'Women's group development from a relational model and a new look at facilitator influence on group development' in M.B. Cohen and A. Mullender (eds) *Gender and Groupwork*. London: Routledge, pp. 16–31.

Simon, S.R. and Stauber, K.W. (2011) 'Technology and groupwork: a mandate and an opportunity', *Groupwork*, 21 (3): 7–21.

Steinberg, D.M. (2004) *The Mutual-aid Approach to Working with Groups: Helping People Help One Another* (2nd edn). London: Haworth Press.

Sullivan, N.W., Mesbur, E.S. and Lang, N.C. (2009) 'Groupwork history: past, present, and future', in A. Gitterman and R. Salmon (eds) *Encyclopedia of Social Work with Groups*. Abingdon, Oxon: Routledge. pp. 1–6.

Tew, J. (2013) 'Theories of empowerment' in M. Davies (ed.) *The Blackwell Companion to Social Work* (4th edn). Oxford: Blackwell.

Thompson, N. (2009) *People Skills* (3rd edn). Basingstoke: Palgrave Macmillan.

Thompson, N. (2012) *Anti-Discriminatory Practice* (5th edn). Basingstoke: Palgrave Macmillan in conjunction with British Association of Social Workers.

Tosone, C. (2009) 'Psychodynamic model', in A. Gitterman and R. Salmon (eds) *Encyclopedia of Social Work with Groups*. London: Routledge.

Trevithick, P. (2005) 'The knowledge base of groupwork and its importance within social work', *Groupwork*, 15 (2): 80–107.

Tuckman, B. (1965) 'Developmental Sequence in Small Groups', *Psychological Bulletin*, 63: 384–399.

Tuckman, B. and Jensen, M. (1977) 'Stages of Small Group Development', *Group and Organisational Studies*, 2: 419–427.

Vernelle, B. (1994) *Understanding and Using Groups*. London: Whiting and Birch.

Wenger, E. (1998) *Communities of Practice: Learning, Meaning, and Identity*. Cambridge: Cambridge University Press.

Wheelan, S.A. (1990) *Facilitating Training Groups: A Guide to Leadership and Verbal Intervention Skills*. New York: Praeger.

Wheelan, S., Davidson, B. and Tilin, F. (2003) 'Group Development across Time: Reality or Illusion?', *Small Group Research*, 34 (2): 223–245.

Whitaker, D.S. (1992) *Using Groups to Help People*. London: Routledge.

Whitaker, D.S. (2007) *Using Groups to Help People* (2nd edn). London: Routledge.

Wonnacott, J. (2012) *Mastering Social Work Supervision*. London: Jessica Kingsley.

Younghusband, E. (Chair) (1959) *Report of the Working Party on Social Workers in the Local Authority Health and Welfare Services*. London: HMSO.

INDEX